Second Edition

# Checklist for Change

## *A Pragmatic Approach to Creating and Controlling Change*

**Thomas R. Harvey**

The Scarecrow Press, Inc.
A Scarecrow Education Book
Lanham, Maryland, and London
2001
Originally published 1995
Technomic Publishing Co, Inc.
Lancaster, Pennsylvania

SCARECROW PRESS, INC.
A Scarecrow Education Book

Published in the United States of America
by Scarecrow Press, Inc.
4720 Boston Way, Lanham, Maryland 20706
www.scarecroweducation.com

4 Pleydell Gardens, Folkestone
Kent CT20 2DN, England

The Technomic edition of this book was catalogued as follows by the Library
of Congress:
Main entry under title:
    Checklist for Change: A Pragmatic Approach to Creating and Controlling
Change – Second Edition
A Technomic Publishing Company book
Bibliography: p.
Includes index p. 175
Library of Congress Catalog Card No. 95-60681
ISBN No. 1-56676-281-2

©™ The paper used in this publication meets the minimum requirements of
American National Standard for Information Sciences—Permanence of
Paper for Printed Library Materials, ANSI/NISO Z39.48–1992.
Manufactured in the United States of America.

*To John and Scott,*
*who have more years to create change than I,*
*and more heart than most.*

**PART III: MANAGING CHANGE TEAMS**

A Chinese fable tells of the emperor who offered his condemned prisoners a choice. They could either be shot by a firing squad or go through a black door. As each prisoner came forward, he chose the firing squad and shunned the black door. At the end of the day, one of the emperor's servants asked him, "Your greatness, may I inquire? What lies beyond the black door?" To which the emperor replied, "Freedom."

The unknown is fearsome to most of us. In the face of change, not knowing what lies beyond, we feel a sense of both dread and awe. This book is dedicated to those caught in just that dilemma. It is written both for those few who are eager for change, and would choose the black door every time, and for the rest of us, who too often opt for the firing squad. This book will help managers and subordinates alike learn about creating change more effectively and efficiently. It is a straightforward conversation about strategies that prove useful to people in getting done the things they believe ought to be done.

In the days of the mythical emperor, the black door raised the ominous specter of the spirits of the beyond. Superstition impelled his prisoners to choose the firing squad. Our problem is not superstition, but lack of the *skills* to mold the unknown. I believe that most managers would opt for change if they were better at creating it. This book is aimed at exactly that—helping you to master the *how* of making the *what* happen.

The change process has been a source of fascination for me for over twenty years. I have studied it, consulted about it, taught it. My ideas are the products of many friends, colleagues, and mentors. First of all, I want to thank my graduate students at Syracuse University, Claremont Graduate School, and, especially, the University of La Verne for their interchange and refining of my ideas. Their thoughts have been invaluable to my thinking. I also want to thank my colleagues at the University of La Verne for their commitment to collaboration and their fundamental belief in change. They, more than most, exemplify effective change.

I also want to thank two of many mentors—Maurice Troyer and Harold Hodgkinson. Maurice Troyer was my graduate professor and the wise old Asian seer each of us should have. He was a mentor who taught me that I was all right even when I failed. Hodgkinson, on the other hand, doesn't even know me. Nevertheless, he first introduced me to change and became my role model for presenting the issue. He is an extraordinary academic with a searing intellect.

My acknowledgements also extend to three lifelong friends who taught me much about change. Ray Sass taught me the importance of the strength of commitment: "Change only occurs when you believe in your capacity to do it." He always believed.

Charlie Johns showed me the value of focusing on the needs of others, rather than the self: "Change occurs when you meet the needs of the changees."

And Biff Green, the best friend and colleague of all, has reinforced for me the power of joyful environments: "Change happens when people are filled with excitement and enthusiasm for the change."

And last, but of course not least, I want to acknowledge my family. They have had to put up with twenty years of my stories and my speeches. They have heard them over and over and have not complained—at least, not too often. They have been the joy of my life and the reason for my belief in change. In their eyes I see hope and faith. And where there is hope and faith, there is change.

Joy, hope, faith, commitment, and experience have all brought me to this place—to write a book about change. I hope it is helpful to you; I hope it provides you with greater skills in creating change. Everyone should have a chance, at least once in a lifetime, to write such a personal preface. Thank you for reading this far and for sharing with me the names of those who have made my life rich. Please continue and join me in this conversation about change.

# PART I

# BACKGROUND FOR CHANGE

# CHAPTER 1

# Introduction

THIS book is addressed to those charged with creating and controlling change. The intent is not to create awareness, for if you are intrigued by the title of this book, you already know that change is important. You have already experienced the singular fascination and frustration associated with creating change in organizations. You already know the hassle and confusion of juggling the changes thrust upon you—by government, by CEO's, by the public, by the vicissitudes of economics, and by anyone who has a new hotshot idea. You also know that change pops up among the top three priorities in almost every survey of management training needs.

Neither is the intent to announce new information about change. Rather, I wish to convey existing knowledge so that you can use it. This book is targeted to all of you, managers and subordinates, who need to know

*How to create change
with a simple,
but systematic,
step-by-step process
that increases your chance for long-term success.*

And that is exactly the premise of this book. The change strategies described herein are, first of all, simple.

## A SIMPLE PROCESS

Management, contrary to some beliefs, is not like nuclear physics. That is, management is not a complex, esoteric, abstract field of knowledge composed of incredibly sophisticated algorithms. Rather, management is simple. It is simple because it consists largely of common

3

sense—occasionally informed by empirical research. Management of change is simple, too, even though the environment is not. Complex demands and events bombard us. New ideas, possibilities, threats, and demands cascade over us as we live in this, a more turbulent organizational time than any other in the recent past. But management must not—and need not—become more abstract or conceptually complex to resolve that turbulence. For if people believe that a task is difficult and complex, they will typically avoid it or do it badly. Conversely, if they believe that a task is easy and understandable, they will more likely tackle it and do it well. Successful management is essential if we are to handle the complexities of our world, and simplicity facilitates success.

Simplicity can be achieved. For example, I remember twenty years ago when I first learned the Statistical Package for the Social Sciences (SPSS). A course in statistics creates high anxiety for most students. Combining statistics with computers often itensifies that anxiety to fever pitch. But we had a wonderful manual called *The Simpleton's Guide to SPSS*. As I remember, it started out saying, "Now look, simpleton, that thing before you is a computer . . ." and proceeded as a thoroughly irreverent, but delightfully simple, guide to the use of SPSS. With that guide, I learned to use the software in twenty to thirty minutes, and I left the computer center thoroughly impressed with that writer's ability to take the complex and make it simple.

Simplicity is equally possible in management. People can do something about that which is direct, straightforward, and simple. They can't implement that which most of us have trouble understanding. The more important the administrative domain, the more imperative that we keep it simple. Just think, if budgets, performance appraisals, strategic planning, or the like were kept simple and straightforward, how much easier it would be to manage your organization. Just think how much better it would be if strategies for change were kept simple, were set out systematically.

## A SYSTEMATIC PROCESS

Something simple is not necessarily easy. To be a good spouse does not involve highly technical skills; nevertheless, many of us do it badly. Driving a car does not require inordinate mental acumen—if you doubt me, just look at any teenage driver. (My own teenage son is the scourge of every parking lot. He is very careful to consult his rearview mirror, but only *after* backing up. If he were more systematic, he would look in the mirror *before* backing up and avoid making our local garage rich.) Although driving is not really a complex skill, tens of thousands of accidents occur yearly—not just because people lack driving skills, but because they do not use the skills they have in an attentive and orderly fashion. To be systematic is to anticipate situations and prepare for them step by step.

## A STEP-BY-STEP PROCESS

The key to being systematic is remembering to do important steps and to do them in order. If management is remarkably less demanding than brain surgery, then why do so many of us do it badly? Because we don't think in advance of the various steps we need to take and then follow through in a logical and orderly progression. We either do not know or do not apply a step-by-step approach to anticipate and plan for problems and opportunities. That is why Chapter 4, the core of this book, is presented as a checklist, a step-by-step approach to change. Indeed, much of this book is presented in list format. Copy the checklists, post them on your bulletin board, follow the procedures step by step, and change will become far more manageable! These checklists increase your chances of success.

## INCREASED CHANCE FOR SUCCESS

No matter what anyone tells you, change is not a science. It has no nomothetic relationships. It has no absolute laws. It is rather, a domain of probabilities, a game of chance. Following the right strategies does not guarantee that you will be successful—just that you are *more likely* to be successful.

Most readers of this book are already fairly successful at change. That is why they are fascinated with the subject. My intent is to make you better change agents. I hope to raise your odds from 60/40 to 75/25 or 85/15. But change strategies are not automatic pilot systems that run themselves; if they were, computers would be great change agents. No, the human qualities of daring, instinct, and intuition are powerful elements in the process. This book does not tackle those personal qualities, but it sets the framework within which those qualities may be applied—a launching pad for innovation and creativity. A firm, systematic base, such as presented here, is your best bet for success.

## LONG-TERM SUCCESS

The strategies for short-term success are much more varied than those for long-term success. Lying, backstabbing, misinforming, and threats, for instance, are all effective ways of getting something done in the near term, but both empirical and intuitive evidence suggest that these strategies hurt us in the long run. People who have been deceived find ways to get even, although revenge may take time.

Strategies for long-term success build upon trust. To be trusted, you must be trustworthy. You will obtain buy-in only to the extent that you trust others to share in choosing, developing, implementing, and/or evaluating an innovation.

If your interest is merely in short-term gain, then the steps described in this book require more effort than you need to put out. If, on the other hand, you seek both long-term survival and personal satisfaction from your change efforts, then the following chapters will prove invaluable.

## TONE OF THE BOOK

If you have not already sensed it, let me emphasize the tone of this book. It is conversational and irreverent and direct and simple. This is not a tome that crystallizes the array of literature on change or marvels at the elegance of change models. This book is a straightforward conversation about change. It is based on nearly two decades' experience in consulting with schools, businesses, hospitals, and other organizations and in teaching graduate students about change.

*Checklist for Change* is intended for managers of all kinds of organizations. It includes examples drawn from businesses, schools and universities, hospitals, and other institutional settings. Too often the literature separates us, I believe, when it should emphasize the commonalities across our organizations. While the nomenclature varies from one setting to another, the dynamics of change do not. My hope is that you will appreciate not only change, but how it occurs in organizations other than your own.

I will be happy if you enjoy reading the book and understand change a bit better. I will be even happier if you pull out the checklists and pin them over your desk to remind you that this simple, systematic, step-by-step process will increase your chances for successful long-term change.

## ORGANIZATION OF CHAPTERS

This book is divided into three parts. Part I deals with issues of change and change strategies. Part II discusses the Change Checklist. It outlines strategies to institutionalize change and to avoid becoming a victim of inappropriate change efforts. Finally, Part III depicts approaches to managing teams in the change process and suggests the relationship between change and three fundamental management functions: evaluation, strategic planning, and budgeting. The book closes with four caveats, two exercises that develop change skills and insights, and a description of bibliographic resources.

# CHAPTER 2

# Twelve Pieces of Folk Wisdom
# about Change

EVERY self-respecting book about management strategies opens with a chapter describing the theoretical domain. Typically, the author presents hundreds of citations, a few charts, and at least one matrix depicting the interrelationships among theorists. Since this volume is only semi-self-respecting, all that will be omitted. Excellent summaries of the theory of change may be found in Bennis et al. (1985), Zaltman et al. (1977), or Lippitt et al. (1985). Turn to them if you want a theoretical base for the pinup checklists that follow. Here, rather than a traditional approach to theory, twelve pieces of folk wisdom about change are presented.

But why folk wisdom? Because folk wisdom captures the essence of experience. For example, some years ago I came upon a wonderful truism by Peter Rossi, "No good evaluation goes unpunished." This irreverent piece of folk wisdom was handed down as a warning to fellow evaluators that the business of making judgments creates backlash. Rossi was arguing that to be right is not always to be loved. His folksy statement renders a powerful truth about evaluation and the people who practice it.

I wish to suggest to you some equally powerful statements about change. These bits of folk wisdom about change undergird the chapters to follow.

## 1. THE GRASS IS ALWAYS GREENER ON THIS SIDE
## OF THE FENCE

Many of us suppose that most people, and particularly Americans, are impelled by wanderlust, an urge for change and innovation. But this is simply not true. People do not yearn to jump the fence into the next pasture, however green.

Rather, resistance to change is inherent in people. They would rather have things stay the same; they are comfortable with the familiar. The literature on change refers to this factor as habit or inertia or the urge for the *status quo*. But I do not like any of these terms because they carry a perjorative connotation—that people are bad for resisting change, that resisters are "sticks-in-the-mud" or "fuddy-duddies" or "reactionaries."

But what others say about us when we resist change is not nearly as bad as what we say to ourselves. I remember discussing resistance to change during a workshop on computer education. I spied a woman in the back of the room with her hands over her eyes. I assumed she was dozing, but a few moments later when she removed her hands, I saw that she was crying. At the break I approached her, and she said:

> What you said about resistance to change being natural and okay was wonderful. I just got divorced and my friends all want me to go out socially, but I have resisted. I don't feel ready to date yet, but I have felt terrible for resisting. I have felt like I was awful for not wanting to do what they suggested. But *it's okay to resist. I'm not a bad person after all.*

Indeed she was not a bad person. The next week I saw her in a follow-up workshop and she smiled, "I went out on a date last night." By accepting resistance as natural and reasonable, she was able to avoid being blocked by guilt or irrelevant issues. She was able to change when there was payoff for her. All of us must recognize that resistance is not bad, but reasonable. We will change when there is sufficient reason, a payoff, to do so.

Payoff—that is the key! One indicant of insanity is engaging in self-abusive acts. We are self-abusive and, hence, partially insane when we do things that have no payoff. It is natural and, indeed, sane to resist something until there is clear payoff for doing it.

In essence, change is not the problem of the chang*ee*, but of the chang*er*. The changer is the one seeking to create change, while the changee needs to be changed to accomplish the outcome. By definition, then, the changer has more to gain and, hence, more responsibility than his counterpart, the changee. The changer is responsible to find payoff for the object of the change effort. The changee has no need and no responsibility to seek out his or her own payoff.

If there is no payoff, then the changee should resist. Think of it! Someone asks you to take on an added duty. This duty will take more of your time and energy and increase your chances of making mistakes (because it is something you have not done before). On top of that, this changer tells you there is no payoff for you. Then you are expected to say, "Great! When do I start?"

Why is the change agent surprised when you resist? Because he or she does not really understand change. You resist because you are sane. You stay right here until you know life is better over there. You greet with skepticism a promise that things might be better, or will be better, in the future. You assume the grass is greener on this side of the fence until you *know* it is greener over there. Let me pose two examples of this reality:

(1) One would expect battered women to leave their homes the first chance they get. However, research on battered women shows that they stay in their abusive settings because they fear the alternatives. They know the demon inside, but they do not know what is outside. In the face of that unknown, they stay where they are. In fact, many battered women remarry into new abusive relationships. Counselors try desperately to make these women aware of the payoffs from alternatives to abuse—to show them that the grass is greener on the other side of the fence—to no avail.

(2) The historiography of the American frontier does not show American thirst for the new and exciting. Rather, the opposite was true. Speculators and land developers took the lead in expanding vistas beyond the Mississippi. They settled an area, cleared it, and then, as soon as things were safe (at least in relative terms), they urged "pioneers" to come West. The speculators then moved on to the new frontier. A few Americans saw money to be made, but most waited to move until everything was O.K.

Most of us do not seek out change. We understand the payoff for the known; we are not aware of the payoff for the unknown. We resist the less known. Therefore, rather than seeing resistance as negative, you would do better to accept it as a state of nature. People resist change unless there is a clear payoff to them. Those last two words must be emphasized—*to them*. The payoff to you as changer is irrelevant; rather, the payoff to the changee must be considered. If resistance is natural, then the changer should accept it—not be put off. People will change when you provide them with a good enough reason to do so. Payoff is necessary to get the changee to jump over the fence.

At this point, it is critical to understand that the payoff must be positive. In other words, the changee must perceive point B as a place to go

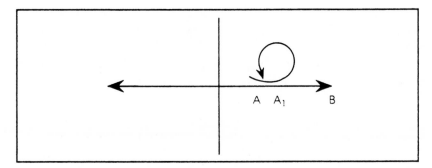

*Figure 2.1. Valence phenomenon.*

toward and not only experience point A as a place to leave. For if you simply deny a given point A, you are left with 360 possible directions in which to go, with the result that changees tend to return to a point $A_1$, close to where they began (see Figure 2.1).

The Russian and French Revolutions are classic examples of focusing on what people wanted to get rid of rather than what they hoped to gain. The French wanted to get rid of the despotic regime of Louis XVI, but in his place they got Robespierre and his reign of terror, and shortly thereafter, Napoleon. Neither were any improvement over the monarchy. The Russians sought to overthrow the czar, and in his place they got Lenin and then Stalin, an archetypal evil figure. Focusing solely on what you don't want seldom yields greener pastures.

The American Revolution, conversely, is a classic example of affirming what was wanted. Our Declaration of Independence focused on what we wanted and created a strategic vision of where we were headed. An imperative for change is to define what you want to get, not what you want to get rid of.

## 2. GUESS WHAT, NOT EVERYONE IS LIKE ME

This aphorism seems to cite the obvious, but it is frequently violated. So often, when we try to describe payoffs for a change effort, we summon up all of its wonderful benefits and advantages to us as changers.

To illustrate this point, let me describe an experiment I have done over 150 times in the past twenty years (Harvey, 1979a) (see Appendix A). I begin this experiment by asking "Who likes buttermilk?" and "Who hates buttermilk?" I pick one person for each response and then ask the buttermilk-lover to convince the buttermilk-hater to drink buttermilk. (What would your strategy be?)

A fascinating interchange follows. I will not go into all that transpires; you can read that elsewhere (Harvey, 1979b). But who do you think does most of the talking? That's right, the changer, the buttermilk-lover. He says that buttermilk is low in calories, is nutritional, tasty, etc. What he does not do is to ask questions. He does not identify the changee's payoffs for change. He just recites a litany of reasons why the changee should drink the buttermilk. And his arguments usually miss the mark.

One of my favorite exchanges occurred between a bounteous board of education member originally from the Deep South and a male California school administrator. She was trying her best to convince him to drink the buttermilk.

> Buttermilk is wonderful, honey. I remember as a child taking corn pone and dippin' it into buttermilk. I would pull it out of the glass and it would have those wonderful lumps of milk all over it.

At that point, half the people in the room felt nauseous. For people who hate buttermilk, that image was not very appealing. But the southern lady thought her argument was captivating. She missed her mark because she assumed that her experiences, drives, and tastes were replicated in the changee. Obviously, they were not.

One of the first prescriptions I give managers interested in change is, "Don't just do something, but stand there!"

That is to say, try to create change only after you have taken time to find out what the other person thinks and feels. Start by asking questions, not giving answers.

(Exercise 2 in Appendix A provides good practice in asking appropriate questions. This exercise leads groups to shorten their decision-making time and increase long-term success with change.)

Because not everyone is the same, asking questions is a key skill in setting the stage for change. For instance, as of this writing, one-third of all Americans do not remember a time when men had not walked on the moon; one-half of Americans are too young to remember the assassination of John F. Kennedy. For me, those riveting events are unforgettable. I know exactly where I was at both of those moments and can easily summon up both the joy and the anguish I felt then. But not everyone is the same. Our experiences, needs, and drives do not inform us about others. So to understand them and find the payoffs that will motivate them to change, we must ask questions. Change is best facilitated with questions, not statements.

## 3. STRESS IS FERTILE GROUND FOR SUCCESS

Change requires stress and strain. If there is no strain in the system, there is no change. Several examples demonstrate this fact.

First, learning theory tells us that curiosity and anxiety are necessary preconditions to learning. Without curiosity or anxiety—in other words, if people feel they know all they need to know—then no learning will take place.

Second, in physical systems, strain is necessary for the development of musculature. Running, exercise, and workouts create strain to enhance physical development. Too great a strain leads to a hernia. Conversely, too little exercise or strain leads to flab and deterioration. America is replete with both extremes. The middle of the road, or eustress, is healthy stress that fosters proper systemic growth.

Third, nearly every invention is a product of stress, a response to inadequacy. The cotton gin was invented to solve problems of cotton production. The light bulb responded to the need for better illumination. Hospitals were created to respond to public health problems. Without stress, there is no invention. Conversely, successful inventions relieve stress and facilitate growth.

The same reality applies to change. If you want to create change, the changee must experience some stress. Take two examples. First, consider this reaction from a parts expediter to whom you propose a new, computerized warehouse inventory system:

> Look, I've been here 22 years. I was here before you came and I'll be here after you're gone. In fact, I've got two years, two months, one week, and six hours before I retire. You can do whatever you want with that change. But I'm not going to do anything different.

Here is a person with low stress—a poor candidate for change.

Conversely, you propose to a first-year teacher that she try a new approach to reading. She says, somewhat hysterically:

> Look, I'm barely surviving as it is. I've got a new class, new grade level, new school, and now you want me to try another new curriculum. On top of all that, I just barely passed the CBEST exam to get this job.

Here is a person with psychic hernia! This teacher's stress level is too high to permit her to cope with any change. In the case of the parts expediter, you must create some stress. In the case of the teacher, you need to lower stress. Neither one can change at the present stress level.

Stress can be divided into three levels:

(1) Low/no stress

(2) Eustress (healthy stress)

(3) Distress

Levels one and three are the ones that need to be managed. If stress is too low, it must be created to induce change; if it is too high (distress), it must be reduced to allow change to occur. Most managers assume that the preponderance of their employees are in level three, overstressed. This is simply not true. There are more than twice as many employees at level one as at level three. Just because there are complaints about the stress of the job does not mean an employee is distressed; he may be in eustress but not like it. Remember, level one is always more comfortable. We'd all rather be there. Comfort, however, is the enemy of change. If I'm sitting on the couch with my channel changer, I'm not about to go out eagerly and mow the lawn. Comfort takes priority over work.

This is probably one of the most misunderstood elements of change. We too often think of stress as bad, as something to eliminate from our organization. The opposite is true. Healthy stress, eustress, is necessary for growth.

Equally, stress and its management are very important to successful change. That is why we have come to recognize in recent years that conflict in organizations is productive. Conflict, used effectively, provides the stress necessary for organizational change and growth. Thus, conflict and stress are not to be avoided but are to be managed intelligently. Remember, comfort is the enemy of change.

## 4. YOU CAN'T MAKE IT IF YOU BELIEVE YOU'RE FAKING IT

Clance (1986), in her fascinating little book entitled *The Imposter Phenomenon*, reports that about 70 percent of all managers believe that they got their position by faking it, that they are really quite mediocre, and that they are lucky that no one has caught them out (so far). At five o'clock each day the manager stares at his or her watch and says,

"Thank God, I got through another day without anyone figuring out what I don't know." If you believe that about yourself, you will find it tough to create change. If you have no faith in your current skills and knowledge, how can you look to learning more? Adding new areas will only increase the probability of getting caught at incompetence. Belief in oneself is the foundation of change.

Let me show how this notion combines with payoff and stress in the work of Kurt Lewin (1951), the father of the modern change theory. Lewin hypothesized that if you are at a given point A and want to go to point B, the change process consists of three parts:

(1) Unfreezing from point A

(2) Moving to point B

(3) Refreezing at point B (see Figure 2.2)

The third phase, *refreezing,* is very easy. People in change do not obey that part of the law of inertia that says that an object in motion tends to continue that motion. Just the opposite—changees readily hunker down in a new spot. Their major problem is backsliding, and that is the issue of institutionalizing change (to be discussed in Chapter 6). Refreezing occurs without any particular strategy on our part.

The middle phase, *moving,* does call for strategic planning and alternatives (see Chapter 10). However, while an important phase, moving is not the critical dilemma in change since once the object of change is unfrozen, change follows quite easily.

Movement is a function of having someplace to go and the skills to move there. Fullan (1991) describes the process of change implementa-

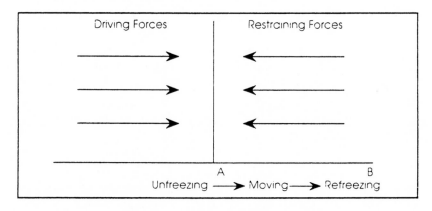

*Figure 2.2. Lewin's force field model.*

tion in his excellent volume, *The New Meaning of Educational Change.* Chapter 6 of this book will also highlight the key institutional factors involved in moving and refreezing. Suffice it to say, moving is not the key dilemma of organizational change.

Unfreezing, on the other hand, is the central challenge. How do you get someone who is settled in place to move off that spot? Frohman's (1970) research gave the best response to that question. He found three fundamental preconditions to unfreezing:

(1) Strain

(2) Valence

(3) Potency

When all three are present, unfreezing is possible.

I have already discussed strain and valence in Folk Wisdom 3 and 1, respectively. Folk Wisdom 3 reminded us that without stress or strain, systems cannot change or grow. Folk Wisdom 1 showed that payoff, which is synonymous with positive valence, is also critical.

The third precondition for unfreezing is potency—you can change only if you believe you can. This is the point of Folk Wisdom 4. If someone wants to teach me tennis and I demur that I am too slow or too fat or too old or too anything, then I guarantee I will never learn tennis. If you say you can't fight city hall, then you can't. If you say to your spouse, "That's just the way I am. You married me that way. I can't change," then you won't. If you say, "You can't teach an old dog new tricks," then the dog will remain safe and comfortable with his old tricks. A splendid old adage says, "If you say you can, or if you say you cannot, you are right." Change will occur only if changees believe that they have the potency to change. People who lack faith in self, people who believe they survive by faking it, are not likely to unfreeze. Therefore, building confidence is an important element in creating change.


## 5. IF THEY HAVEN'T BOUGHT IT, THEY AREN'T GOING TO KEEP IT

It is one thing to move folks from point A to point B; it is another to keep them there. For example, as of the writing of this book, I have the delight of being an elected official in the small California city of La Verne. Whenever we have a proposal to build apartments in residential neighborhoods, we have residents who strongly oppose that construction. The homeowners complain that renters do not maintain their property as well as homeowners – that they do not paint, mow, water, or prune as diligently. Research supports these complaints. What you don't own, you don't care for as well.

The same is true in management. Programs or procedures that employees do not own, they will not maintain. What, then, is the single best predictor of ownership? Participation!

When people are involved in a program, they own it. Conversely, if they are handed a program without any involvement, they will not mow, paint, or prune it. That is why collaborative strategies (to be discussed in more detail in Chapter 9) are so critical to successful change. Collaboration sets the stage for effective implementation and for institutionalization of change. If you want change to last, get people involved.

## 6. PUSH ME AND I'LL PUSH YOU BACK

Hold up your hand. Have someone push on it. What do you do? You push back.

To resist force is a natural biological reflex. Coercion increases resistance. If you are strong enough, you can overcome resistance, but do not be mistaken about the outcome. Resistance does not dissolve; it merely goes underground – and that is where it is most dangerous. This piece of folk wisdom has an important corollary: People have an infinite capacity to wait to get even.

Resistance that has been overpowered and driven underground will reappear some other time or place when least expected. Some innocuous issue will generate significant resistance, and you will wonder why. The real source is not this new issue but, rather, one that has been festering for a month, a year, or three years. The underground resistance you created in the past bears fruit in the present. Coercive strategies for change increase generalized resistance and, thus, decrease the probability of successful long-term change.

Let me place this push/push back aphorism in the context of change theory generally. Bennis' (1985) classic book on change describes three basic change strategies:

(1) Power-coercive

(2) Rational-empirical

(3) Normative-reeducative[1]

While there are other taxonomies, this one works as well as any.

Power-coercive strategies are "push" strategies—for example, authoritative command ("I'm your boss, do it!"), guilt, voting, and the like. These strategies are the fastest and most efficient in the short term, but they depend on your power. They are short-term strategies because they increase resistance and sow the seeds of your ultimate downfall.

Rational-empirical strategies assume that people change through rational response to new knowledge or data. But research suggests that rational approaches, while the most commonly used strategies, are the *least* effective (Hodgkinson, 1971). How many times have you seen wonderfully reasoned arguments and studies effect change? Seldom, if you are in the mainstream of management. Few human beings change solely because of data or evidence. There are, indeed, settings and individuals for which rational approaches work, but in most cases they do not.

Pfeffer (1981) suggests that rational strategies work under three conditions:

(1) Plentiful resources

(2) Clear, unambiguous goals

(3) No conflict over priorities

If all three are present, then data and evidence will work. In fact, if you are a member of such an organization, any strategy will work! It is, indeed, the absence of such conditions that thwarts efforts at change. Because these three conditions so rarely exist together, rational change strategies are seldom effective.

Smoking may be the most glaring example of the inefficacy of rational arguments in changing behavior. When the Surgeon General issued his reports on the negative impact of smoking on health, people generally agreed, but their habits changed very little. In fact, in the months following the early reports, the incidence of smoking increased. If smoking is any indicator, we do well to turn to other, nonrational strategies to effect long-term change.

---

[1]For a full description see Chin and Benne (1985).

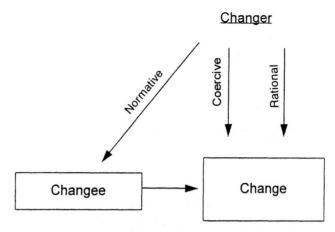

*Figure 2.3.* Change strategies.

The third category, normative-reeducative change strategies, links a change to people's needs and drives. These are the strategies that search for payoff for the change, thus, focusing on the changee. In the first two approaches, attention is concentrated on the change itself. In the normative-reeducative approach, it is directed toward the changees, linking their needs and drives with the change (see Figure 2.3).

The advantage of normative approaches is that they have the greatest long-range impact. Their disadvantage is that they take more effort and time. In both of these ways they are like positive reinforcement strategies in psychology.

Now, back to "Push me and I'll push you back." The fundamental thrust of this piece of folk wisdom is that change agents must pick their strategies carefully. Coercion is efficient but creates backlash; rational strategies are comfortable but largely ineffective; normative strategies are the most effective but take the most effort and self-discipline. Each has its advantages and disadvantages; each should be used when most appropriate. When long-term commitment is needed, normative strategies work best. When time is of the essence, coercive strategies are in order. But remember to watch for the push back.

## 7. IF YOU WANT CHANGE, HAVE A PARTY

So often change efforts are sold as important, serious, and indispensable. Changes are described in ponderous, awesome terms. No wonder they come across as heavy and boring. This is exactly the wrong tack to take.

People love parties; they love having a good time. We all define "party" differently, but we thirst for enjoyment and excitement. When we link change with gravity, we increase resistance. When we link it with excitement and joy, people want to join. All you need do is think about the classic phrase, "Jump on the bandwagon." A bandwagon sounds exciting and fun. Have you ever heard anyone say "I want to jump on a hearse?" Of course not!

This party imperative means that retreats and social gatherings, cocktail parties and lunches, are ripe occasions for introducing changees to new ideas. These occasions should be exploited to their fullest. I am always amazed by the CEO who takes his or her staff on a retreat to a wonderful mountain or seashore setting and then keeps them in sessions morning, noon, and night. He believes (or his board insists that he believe) that only meeting time is productive, that having fun is nonproductive. This attitude shows limited insight into the change process. When people are having a good time, they are more open to new possibilities. [For examples of celebration and joy inducers, see Harvey and Drolet (1994)].

## 8. 100 PROOF CHANGE, LIKE 100 PROOF WHISKEY, IS HARD TO STOMACH

Change strategists are too often dominated by an either-or mentality: "If I don't get all that I asked for, then I've failed." Many a manager offers a lyric argument for change, lays out a magnificent strategy, and then feels crushed when the changees, in word or in deed, say, "I'll think about it!" Think about it? You expect the changees to fall to their knees in some incredible conversion crisis and accept the overwhelming and obvious necessity of the proposed change. Instead, they say they will think about it!

In reality, most change efforts do not achieve 100 proof success. The higher your change expectation, the more likely you will experience failure or disappointment. Instead, realize that 60 percent, or 50 percent, or even 30 percent achievement of what you proposed is success. Most changees cannot stomach a change in its totality. Like the buttermilk tester, they may sip; they simply cannot drink the whole glass. To be realistic, accept 60 proof change.

For example, I remember confronting my son with my need for him to keep his room neater. I lectured him on the importance of order and cleanliness. The first week was great. Then each ensuing week he got worse, to the point where he had a clean room about 50 percent of the time. My fundamental urge was to criticize him for not cleaning his room half the time, but then I realized that he had changed. He was now actually *cleaning* it 50 percent of the time. I needed to appreciate his progress, his partial approximation of the change I sought, not scold him for the part not yet achieved.

For another example, this time about management, I remember about fifteen years ago being asked as a manager to implement a new quality assurance system for a university. While there was much resistance, we successfully got the various departments to accept the new program and course evaluation system, at least most of the time. At the end of the year, I audited the process and found a number of courses that were not revised according to "my" system. I railed at my colleagues and harangued them about their oversights. Then, I realized that I was focusing on the 20 percent of the change that had not succeeded and ignoring the 80 percent that had. This is not to suggest that we should ignore the shortfalls of change, but simply that we must recognize change does not occur all at once. Change comes in stages. Celebrate the success of the early stages and the later stages will emerge.

## 9. CHANGE IS LOSS

It is critical to remember that for every change proposed or achieved, someone loses something. Someone who was served well by the old program will be less well served by the new—or will at least lose the comfort of the old approach. Terry Deal (1982) suggests that we raise a big barrier when we fail to recognize change as loss, as the death of the old. In fact, he proposes literally holding a wake for the old program, project, or whatever is being changed. This ceremony allows the disciples to honor and extol what has gone before and to experience an important phase of the grieving process. The memorial service is then followed by the customary festival or wake, thus, easing the transition to the new.

I do not propose so literal a rendition of the grieving process. But I do underscore the reality that every change you propose causes loss for someone and, hence, every change contains negative elements. If you overlook this, you will simply increase resistance and drive it underground. And, as with push/push back, hidden resistance becomes a genuine danger for your continued leadership. For example, when a hospital creates a new quality circle program, it means the death of the old informal channels of communication; it means loss of some power for middle managers; it means loss of scapegoats.

In another example, when we adopt a new computer system, some feel the loss of old, comfortable manual systems and fear for their jobs. When we downsize (right-size?) organizations, we sever long ties and break old patterns of association. When we create middle schools out of junior high schools, we shatter the known and comfortable and replace it with the unknown and risky.

Change means loss, and changers need to recognize the natural grief and resistance that comes from loss. So, for successful change, allow people to work through their sense of loss.

## 10. YOU LEARN TO WALK ONLY BY TAKING BABY STEPS

A frequent error among change strategists is to attempt too great a change early on. The larger the change effort at the beginning, the lower the chance of long-term success. As you can undoubtedly tell, I believe in old adages, and one of the best is, "Nothing succeeds like success." If you want to increase significant long-term success, make sure people experience numerous small successes along the way—what behaviorists call a successive approximation of success.

You would not expect a first-grader to succeed at multiplication tables. Instead, you teach 1 + 1 and 2 + 2 and 5 + 6, and the like, and reward success at each step of the way. Similarly, if a change requires three years to complete, you must break down the change effort into a series of smaller, incremental changes, each with its indicators of achievement. In fact, you would do well to start with a couple of strawman changes, that is, minor changes that cannot possibly fail, then build into successively larger changes. As your changee learns to take baby steps, each succeeding step can become a bit larger and bolder. This is sometimes called the "theory of small wins"—breaking down long-term objectives into a series of near-term successes.

## 11. TO ERR IS NOT ONLY HUMAN, BUT DIVINE

Barnaby Keeney, a wonderfully impertinent college president during my early faculty years, embodies this precept. In the early 1970s he told the story of his term at the National Endowment for the Humanities (NEH). As the first chairman of the Endowment, he had the "honor" of going to Capitol Hill to give a state-of-the-endowment report to the appropriate senate committee. He talked for about forty-five minutes about NEH's first-year successes. When the committee chairman thanked him, he expressed disappointment because no one had questioned him about his failures. The committee chairman was taken aback and wondered why Keeney was so insistent on detailing his losses. Keeney replied simply, "If I have no failures, then you ought to fire me on the spot, because it means that I'm not trying enough things; I'm not trying to reach beyond my ready grasp." He insisted that the strength of an organization lay in its ability to accept and appreciate failure and error.

You will never fail if you take on easy, routine tasks. But just as a child learns from trying to do more than he has ever tried before, so does an organization. The bold and productive fail more than the timid and mundane, but they also succeed far more. Great leaders demonstrate the capacity to learn from mistakes, not the ability to avoid them. Certainly, we want to win more than we lose, but an environment that supports change is marked by allowing and accepting error as the natural by-product of innovation and risk. Change rarely occurs in organizations where everybody is "covering their butt." Conversely, dynamic environments encourage risk and reward learning from mistakes. They are also much more fun.

## 12. RISK IS NOT RUSSIAN ROULETTE

When groups of managers are asked what qualities typify effective change agents, they almost always list "risk-taker." When asked what this means, responses are heard along the line of "people who are willing to take a chance." The next question is the most interesting, "How much of a chance?" The answer to this question reveals managers' misunderstanding of the reality of risk-taking and what accounts for the effectiveness of risk-takers.

Great entrepreneurs and innovators are *not* high-risk people. Rather, as Drucker's (1985) excellent book on *Innovation and Entrepreneurship* points out, most long-term effective entrepreneurs exercise bounded risk. They know the probability of their success and structure the odds in their favor. They set up trade-offs wherein the gains clearly outweigh the probable losses.[2]

Some high-riskers, on the other hand, are so proud of taking risks that they play with six metaphorical bullets. That's not risk; that is idiocy. With Russian roulette, your long-term survival is extremely limited. So, effective change agents don't play Russian roulette or, at least, the gun is not at *their* head.

Sky diving is one of these wonderfully risky sports. But the risk is bounded. Good, long-lived sky divers check their own parachutes before each jump. They know the limits of height, wind, and cloth. They risk, but they limit or put bounds to the risk. Entrepreneurs who take great chances may produce great one-shot inventions or cash in on a lucky speculation, but they do not experience repeated, long-term success. Bounded risk is the sign of a thriving—and surviving—change agent.

## CONCLUDING NOTE

These, then, are the twelve pieces of folk wisdom that were promised to you. They are listed in Figure 2.4. You may want to add your

---

1. The Grass Is Always Greener on *This* Side of the Fence.
2. Guess What! Not Everyone Is Like Me.
3. Stress Is Fertile Ground for Success.
4. You Can't Make It If You Believe You're Faking It.
5. If They Haven't Bought It, They Aren't Going to Keep It.
6. Push Me and I'll Push You Back.
7. If You Want Change, Have a Party.
8. 100-Proof Change, Like 100 Proof Whiskey, Is Hard to Stomach.
9. Change Is Loss.
10. You Learn to Walk Only by Taking Baby Steps.
11. To Err Is Not Only Human, but Divine.
12. Risk Is Not Russian Roulette.

---

*Figure 2.4.* Twelve pieces of folk wisdom.

[2]For rational decision models that illustrate this, see White et al. (1985) on payoff matrices.

own. The important thing to remember is that we know a great deal about creating change. The checklist presented in Chapter 5 builds upon these precepts. Change is a known domain, even though some practitioners treat it as witchcraft or voodoo. Folk wisdom is okay; witchcraft is not. So let us go on to find out how these twelve precepts operate in practice.

# CHAPTER 3

# Resistance to Change

HAVE you ever proposed a change and found no one opposing you? For many of us the answer is yes. But reflect back upon those occasions. Were you pleased? If the answer is yes yet again, then you have fallen prey to one of the great fallacies about change. For change without resistance is no change at all — it is an illusion of change. When you propose change and receive no resistance, one of four things is true.

(1) Nothing has changed. People were already carrying out your idea in some substantial form or fashion. You may have given it a new name or terminology or exterior, but a rose by any other name is still a rose.

(2) People in your organization are dead from the neck up; they have no interest in new ideas, pro or con. They are organizational zombies.

(3) Everyone thinks alike, so your change strikes everyone in the same way. Because of this group-think, everybody sees your idea as fitting the organization perfectly. Research shows that if this condition describes your workplace, you are probably in trouble in the long run. Lack of resistance for this reason is not a sign of success.

(4) Resistance exists, but no one will say so aloud, at least not in the designated organizational settings. You may overhear the resistance expressed in the parking lot, at the bar, or among the bowling team. In this case, resistance has gone underground, where, as noted in the previous chapter, it is the most dangerous. Submerged resistance manifests itself later, often in guerrilla warfare — hit and pull back, hit and pull back, hit and pull back. Managers seldom win guerrilla wars.

All four of these conditions are real problems for organizations and are to be devoutly avoided. So, my opening prescription to you is:

27

Never again look on the face of change and hope for no resistance. Open resistance gives you a healthy chance to effect long-term change.

Great change agents celebrate resistance. They do not stop in the face of it, but they do try to understand it and encourage honesty. It's a bit like getting up in the middle of the night to go to the bathroom. Your room is pitch dark, and you need to find your way. What do you do? You feel for the edge of your bed or the wall or a desk or a bureau, and then orient yourself. Now you know how to find the bathroom. Resistance is the same. You must understand the shape of the resistance before you can change it. You need to let people be honest about their feelings of resistance so that you can orient yourself and find your way to the change. Great leaders celebrate resistance.

## PAUCITY OF RESEARCH BASE

This pivotal concept of resistance is poorly covered in the literature on change. Writers seldom view resistance as a positive and necessary element in the change process. Sources of resistance are inadequately treated and seldom catalogued in empirical research. [For the best discussion to date, see Odiorne's (1981) *The Change Resisters.*]

Moreover, resistance is too often viewed as a dimension of personality, rather than as a logical consequence of change propositions. Some people are described as "open to change" (these are the good people) and others as "closed to change" (these are the bad people). But in truth, human beings resist change for good and logical reasons. The changer has the need to discover those reasons and deal with them. In other words, resistance is the problem of the changer and *not* the changee. The literature base generally fails to acknowledge that reality. It is in that area of resistance that this book most departs from other theorists on change. The model of change, and its accompanying checklist, is essentially a *resistance-based approach.* This book argues that to be successful at creating and controlling change, you must celebrate resistance. You must understand it, accept it, and use it.

## FORCE FIELD ANALYSIS

As noted earlier, Lewin's (1951) force field analysis fathered much of the modern change theory. His model (shown in Figure 2.2 in Chapter 2) identifies driving forces and restraining forces at loggerheads in every change situation. Therefore, in developing a change strategy, one can:

(1) Increase the drivers

(2) Decrease the restrainers (resisters)

(3) Turn a restrainer into a driver

Alternative three has obvious advantages. But which is a better strategy, one or two? The most common practice is alternative one, to increase the drivers. That is, we find out who supports the change and, through them, try to increase pressure on the resisters. We keep pushing the change until we break down or overpower the resisters. Strikes, petitions, voting, mass protest, and appealing to superiors exemplify alternative one, applying pressure to increase the driving forces.

Most of us approach change in this way. In broad public policy areas, this approach has some probability of working, but for organizations the chance for success is only short-term. (Remember, push me and I'll push you back.) To increase the drivers inevitably increases resistance and propels it to that dangerous underground area.

Therefore, the best choice between alternatives one and two is the latter, to decrease resistance. That strategy avoids backlash and generates greater commitment to implementing the change. But to reduce restrainers (resisters), one must first diagnose what they are.

## SOURCES OF RESISTANCE

Every organization, like every family, is different. So no single set of descriptors will work for all organizations. Nevertheless, a list of the most common sources of resistance follows, along with appropriate antidotes. Your task is to analyze each change episode to see the degree to which each source is operating in your setting and to add other idiosyncrasies that may be pertinent for your time and place. But it is risky to assume the sources of resistance; you must ask questions to find out how the changees feel. Remember, don't just do something, but stand there! To what degree is each of the following elements affecting your change effort?

### *Lack of Ownership*

Changees resist efforts they see as alien, imposed from without. If they lack ownership for the change, they will in all likelihood refuse to go along with it. As noted earlier, the best predictor of ownership is participation, whether that participation relates to defining the change itself or only to its implementation. Involvement at both levels – the what and the how – maximizes chances for change.

Unfortunately, we often receive change demands from others, both above and around us. In these cases we have limited room to define the what of change, but we can define the how. In either case, it is important to make change user-friendly and not alien; to give changees some opportunity for self-determination. Participation in defining how change is to be implemented is a key to overcoming resistance.

For example, California's state legislature in 1983 mandated an array of reforms with few guidelines for implementation. They told schools what to do but not how. Schools that have railed against this imposition have experienced much frustration and failure. However, schools that succeeded did so by actually involving their staff in defining *how* to implement the reforms and *how* to mesh the reforms with their own goals. These schools took the lemons of state mandates and turned them into lemonade for their schools. They created payoff through active participation, by seizing upon the threat-turned-opportunity at hand.

### Lack of Benefits

Perhaps the most common source of resistance to change is lack of payoff. Employees, spouses, friends, and even the saintly resist doing something new if they see no benefits or advantages for themselves. Far too many change proposals are ripe with advantages for the changers and bereft of anything for the changee. Once again, state reforms in education are glorious examples of this reality. Schools are consistently asked to add programs and produce more paper with little or no new resources or psychological payoffs. Yet legislators are surprised when schools either resist or sabotage the effort. How much change would you see if there were no payoffs for changers, either?

Payoffs need not be pecuniary. I remember two of us as junior faculty being asked to teach an overload course for free. I accepted and my close colleague refused. We were both sane in doing so. I was interested in going into administration and wanted to establish my "self-sacrificing" image. My friend was tenured and wanted to teach well the classes he already had. My payoff came with accepting the change; his lay in resisting it. Payoff is not a negative term – it simply fits human nature. We perform those things best that give us rewards in terms of money or satisfaction, self-image, affection, or power. As long as we maintain a long-term perspective on rewards, payoff is a sane and desirable component of change. (See Chapter 4 for detail on payoffs.)

## Increased Burdens

Related to payoffs is the issue of burdens. I have limited time, money, and energy; anything that robs me of these, I will strongly resist. This is a profound dilemma. Virtually every change takes time, money, and energy. Of these, energy and money are expandable and elastic, whereas time is not. So, the most precious and jealously guarded of the three is time.

We all have the same amount of time and can gain no more. If your change effort will reduce the burdens – save money, replenish energy, or reduce wasted time – then it will be eagerly pursued. But if it consumes these resources, the only sane response is to resist. Thus, even though change consumes time, money, and/or energy, the net effect must be to reduce burdens. Otherwise, it is likely to be resisted.

## Lack of Top-Brass Support

"We'd like you to try this new approach, but we can't guarantee that the top brass will be supportive." Does that sound like a great deal? The fact is that most employees will not effect change unless they believe that those vested with responsibility for organizational goals also support the change. This runs counter to the notion that much change is grassroots change – that it swells up from the lowest levels of the organization. Occasionally grassroots change occurs, but typically, the commitment of managers at upper levels is critical to the commitment of managers throughout the organization. Top-brass support is necessary, but not sufficient, to a successful change effort.

This is not to say that advocates for a change must always include the heads of organizations, but the role of CEO's and/or their "lieutenants" is critical to effective change. Before proceeding, change agents need to garner understanding, commitment, and resources from leaders in the organization.

## Loneliness

People need people. Nothing is more intimidating and scary for most changees than to hear, "You're going to be on the cutting edge; no one else has ever tried this. You'll be the pioneer." Few people want to venture into a new world alone. Columbus did not go alone; he had three ships. Lewis had Clark. Even the Lone Ranger had Tonto.

If a change calls on us to leave the collegial cocoon of our peer groups, we resist. The often unspoken response to trying something first is, "How about if I'm the second or third?" Aloud, we ask, "Who else has tried this? Where else has this worked?" True innovation is too lonely for most people. They want company on the road to change.

## Insecurity

Personal and psychic security is a prominent issue in almost every theory of motivation. Researchers from Maslow (1970) to Herzberg et al. (1959) have argued the importance of security. If you propose a change that threatens an individual's security or is merely perceived as threatening, he or she will resist. The drive for survival—physically, mentally, or economically—is more powerful than almost any other drive. Keep in mind that the changer's perception of the security threat is irrelevant; the key lies in how the changees see it. If they feel threatened, then they will resist and fight back. In industry, robotics is a realistic threat to worker security. In education, computers and technology are not realistic threats to job security but they are often seen as such. In both cases employees resist. They foresee loss of their jobs, and resistance will be overcome only by demonstrating that their jobs are secure. Change that enhances security holds a much better chance for success.

## Norm Incongruence

"We don't do it that way around here." These eight words tell you that your change effort has run headlong into the norms of the organization and that you are in trouble. Norms are powerful and tend to overwhelm individual preference (Deal and Kennedy, 1982). The literature on socialization is replete with examples of individual role expectations running into organizational norms, with norms the decided winner (Schein, 1979).

The norms and culture of the organization are customs and practices that have been built up for years. They serve the members' individual needs. They also act as a source of identity and distinction for the organization. They are functional and necessary (Deal and Kennedy, 1982). Change that runs counter to the norms will be resisted by all but a few of the rebels. Wearing blue shirts at IBM won't work. Orderly systems in universities run counter to faculty love of controlled chaos. Accountability to hospital administrators runs counter to physicians' norms of independence and expertise.

If you are in any of these predicaments, you must first work on changing the norms – that is a gargantuan task. An alternative may be to recraft the change to fit more easily into the established culture. Either way, culture is too important to be ignored.

### Boredom

As mentioned in Chapter 2, people love to have parties. They want to enjoy themselves. They will resist ponderous, funereal, and grave depictions of change efforts. Speakers give clear proof of this reality. Do you learn more from speakers who present good content in a mono-tone or from those who offer solid content with a lively sense of hu-mor? The latter, of course. When you laugh during a speech, you find the subject magnetic.

Humor is a magnificent managerial skill because it allows people to enjoy what they are doing. It is alluring, enticing, and thought-provoking. When you make your change effort fun, you will easily garner followers. But when you argue that your proposal will "change the face of management, it is critical, we're in trouble and have to adapt, this change is imperative, etc., etc., etc.,"–then you emphasize the gravity of the change, not its excitement. Grave, ponderous changes are seen as boring and, hence, resisted. While the change may be grave, the joy you convey will be more powerful in creating change than the gravity.

Gravity focuses on what you need to leave behind; joy, on what you want to go toward. As mentioned in Chapter 2, emphasizing point A only guarantees that changees will likely hunker down nearby at point $A_1$. Invest the change episode with your joy and enthusiasm and watch people embrace your idea!

### Chaos

Control is a powerful correlative to security. All you need to do is think of such terms as "out of control," "uncontrolled," or "uncontrol-lable." Any of these epithets undercuts change. For most of us, the issue of control and security is prominent. In change, this problem manifests itself in the need for order and responsibility. When a change project offers the very real possibility of chaos and loss of control, people resist. We summon up terrible images of those things we cannot control and then reject anything that increases the probability of actualizing those images. Conversely, if the change project suggests we will have more control, more accountability, more order, or more authority, then we welcome it with open arms. Change that creates the perception of more control inspires allegiance. "Perception" is the critical word.

### *Superiority*

Too many change efforts are morality plays posing good against evil. "I'm for innovation and goodness and you're for the status quo and evil." While this is obviously hyperbole, the morality play notion does tend to dominate our approach to change. Any of us will resist change from people who tell us—directly or indirectly—that they are superior. Most of us avoid the word "superior," but we communicate our moral superiority in phases like:

- As you become more experienced (AKA mature), you will like my idea.
- Later on, you'll see that I'm just thinking of you.
- If you knew enough, you'd see it my way.
- Try to be more open to change.
- You need to learn to take risks.
- Trust me—I know what's best!

Even children resist such advice! Is it any wonder that adults, too, see through our insistent prodding? We assume that we have a superior idea and then posture accordingly.

It is far better if the manager emphasizes that the new idea is an option, an alternative, that works to solve a problem or satisfy a need. This approach takes the changee at eye level. The changer tries to understand the changee's needs and drives as well as the saneness of reluctance on his or her part. The situation is no longer good versus evil—just colleagues working together to an end. A play on words? Perhaps. But more importantly, a play on psyche. We accept change more easily when we see it at eye level, rather than looking up to understand it.

## *Differential Knowledge*

Information is power. Unequal information translates to unequal power. Unequal power leads to resistance and competition. Not that people rely on information and data to make decisions. Rather, they want to feel informed and knowledgeable about their organization. The underlying issue is inclusion. Have you ever sat in a meeting where someone mentioned a memo that everyone but you had received? Your reaction was probably a blend of surprise and dismay. Suddenly, that memo, which you probably would have ignored anyway, becomes the most important piece of information in the world.

People want to be treated equally and to receive the same information. The "trust me I know more about this than you" approach not only demonstrates lack of empathy, but also signals differential information. Consequently, raised eyebrows will give way to a distinct feeling of distrust. If you want change to occur, be sure that changees have adequate and equal information about the change. Information means inclusion, consideration, and respect. Without these, there is resistance.

## *Lack of Recognition*

I remember vividly the day I was speaking on change to a group of high school teachers in a particular southern California school district. A woman in the front row was knitting away. Every five minutes or so she would turn to one of her neighbors and say in a voice loud enough for all to hear, but not loud enough to disrupt my speech, some version of the following: "That will never work here. We've tried it. He doesn't know us. The stories I could tell. Tsk. Tsk."

She was the Madame DeFarge (see Dickens' *Tale of Two Cities*). Every organization has a Madame or Monsieur DeFarge. They are professional rebels or resisters. They receive organizational recognition by opposing things. They have never met a change that they found irresistible. The often-used strategy of isolation seldom works. It only increases their recognition and, very often, colleagial sympathy. But the issue here is not change; it is recognition.

Therefore, to overcome the Madame DeFarges of the world (and sometimes you can simply ignore them), you must give them recognition. Pfeffer (1981) suggests the term "cooption"—that is, giving them recognition by publicly acknowledging their worth and including them in the change process. By making them part of the solution, you convert opponents into proponents. You do not coopt them solely for political purposes. New ideas, differences of opinion, tough cautions, and honest conflict are productive to decision making and change. You need, and benefit from, your rebels and resisters. So recognize Madame DeFarge by making her a member of your change team.

### Sudden Wholesale Change

Commercials clearly reflect how people act and change. Remember these? "Try it, you'll like it!" "I don't believe I ate the whole thing!" "Just take it for a spin!" All these slogans affirm the same principle: If you want change, do it gradually. People resist large, major, wholesale changes. They want to begin with baby steps. They want just to sip, taste, or try. They don't want to eat the whole thing—it's too much. We have all experienced "experimental" programs that lasted for years, a temporary modular construction that lasted longer than its inhabitants. Gradualism works! Gradualism, or trialism, overcomes natural resistance to massive changes. Help them try a small behavior change, then a bigger one, and a bigger one, etc. Take one small step at a time. Capitalize on the theory of small wins.

### Failure

Nothing promotes failure like failure. How would you react if I said, "Look, I'd like you to try out this new program. We've tried it three times before and no one has made it work. Why don't you give it a try?" It makes you want to rush out and give your all, doesn't it?

Nothing destroys teams like failure. Failure leads to scapegoating, depression, and group dispersion. Yet that is what many managers emphasize. They walk around looking for something wrong. They emphasize what people cannot do. They insist on failure and then wonder why no one wants to risk something new.

Conversely, if I tell you that you are capable and talented and and successful, then how do you react? Your first reaction is, "Boy, you've got good taste!" You are impressed with the fact that I'm impressed with you, and you begin to believe that my opinion is truth. Positive affirmations are not the only kinds of feedback a manager gives, but without them, change is far less likely. People resist the negative. They respond to success and affirmation.

### Extremes of Organizational Structure

Hage and Aiken (1970) have looked at the relationship between organizational centralization, formulation, and stratification on the one hand—and productive, long-term change on the other. My experience confirms these findings. The relationship between change and each of these structural variables is not linear, but curvilinear. Take the variable of centralization, put it on a continuum from highly decentralized to highly centralized and relate that continuum to change. You will see a regression line that looks something like Figure 3.1.

At both ends of the centralization continuum you have low change. High centralization means dominant use of authoritative command and limited participation. This state makes change difficult. Conversely, high *de*centralization yields high autonomy and modestly controlled chaos. Everybody does his own thing, and no one provides direction. This, too, makes change difficult.

The greatest potential for change exists in the middle, where direction and participation are linked. I will discuss this more fully in Chapter 9 when I describe the notion of directive collaboration. Here, I simply emphasize that extreme organizational structures by their nature make resistance more likely and change more difficult. In other words, not only human, but also structural, variables give rise to resistance. It should be added that Figure 3.1 could have been as easily

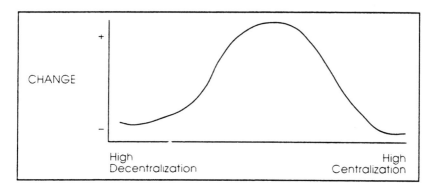

*Figure 3.1. Change and centralization.*

drawn for formalization and stratification with the same regression line. Extremes of structure suppress the probability of change.

### Unique Sources of Resistance

Every organization has unique characteristics that affect change. In questioning and seeking sources of resistance, the changer must be aware of idiosyncratic and unusual factors. Everyone is not like me; moreover, everyone is not like everyone else. You need to add to the list your own array of resistances. What sources of resistance do you see in your organization?

## ANTIDOTES

As you can see in Figure 3.2, for every resistance factor there is an antidote. These antidotes serve as the core of your strategy in overcom-

| Cause | Antidote |
|---|---|
| Lack of ownership | Involvement |
| Lack of benefits | Payoff |
| Increased burdens | Lighten load |
| Lack of top brass support | Top brass support |
| Loneliness | Collegiality |
| Insecurity | Security |
| Norm incongruence | Norm congruence |
| Boredom | Fun |
| Chaos | Control |
| Superiority | Empathy |
| Differential knowledge | Equal information |
| Lack of recognition | Involvement |
| Sudden, wholesale change | Gradualism |
| Failure | Affirmation |
| Extremes of organizational structure | Moderate centralization, formalization, or stratification |
| Unique sources | Unique solutions |

*Figure 3.2. Sources of resistance.*

ing resistance to change. They are probably all self-explanatory, so I will describe each only briefly.

- Involvement—Forming a team and making people part of the process is critical here. This can be done as a whole group, but more likely in small groups with widespread involvement through the accordion process (see Chapter 6).
- Payoff—This antidote calls for the changer to make sure to provide some reward for the changee; this reward must be positive from the perspective of the changee (see Chapter 4).
- Lighten load—The changer should explore what trade-off in time or responsibility can be forged. You cannot just keep adding to people's loads.
- Top-brass support—You need to enlist leader support before proceeding with the change. The support must be clear and overt.
- Collegiality—This is essentially the use of teams for change (see Chapter 8).
- Security—You need to explore the individual's (or individuals') future with the organization. Security may require job redesign or role reevaluation.
- Norm congruence—If you are attacking organizational norms, you will have a double change—the change you were seeking originally, and a norm change. [See Harvey and Drolet (1994) for norm processes.]
- Fun—You should focus on celebrations and joy. What would make this change fun?
- Control—You need to keep the change manageable. Use the theory of small wins.
- Empathy—For this antidote one must focus on three elements: (1) multiple recognition, not just a few changees, (2) feedback on behavior, and (3) encouraging peer-to-peer recognition.
- Equal information—You need to keep everyone equally informed. No secrets!
- Graduation—This is another application of the theory of small wins (see Chapter 4).
- Affirmation—You need to make sure you recognize people for positive contributions. Secondly, you need to see failures as surprises, not personal shortcomings. What happened here that we did not expect? Why?
- Structural moderation—You must examine your organization for extremes of structure and move to the middle ground.

From these general strategies you will build a specific strategy to overcome resistance to change.

## CONCLUDING NOTE

Figure 3.2 summarizes sources of resistance, and Form 5 on page 97 proposes a five-point instrument for assessing their presence. Not all factors operate in every change episode. Any resistance factor with a rating of one or two is not really a problem. Anything with a four or five is definitely a source of resistance to be addressed in your change strategy. Anything with a three deserves continued observation and may be included in secondary strategies.

I strongly urge you to develop your change plan with a team of changers. Involving others is more fun and more productive. As you will discover in succeeding chapters, to begin by assessing sources of resistance is critical to developing a viable plan.

Building a change strategy is not a complex notion. It begins with diagnosis. You must remember to assess the conditions of the changees and then build your strategy from there.

# CHAPTER 4

# Crafting Strategies for Unfreezing

A wise change agent remembers Harvey's 90 percent rule: 90 percent of your time will be spent on the *what* of change; 90 percent of your success will come from the *how* of change. The *what* may determine whether the change matters in the long run but has very little to do with whether the change actually happens.

The power of a good idea is never enough. Rather, strategies – systematic plans for creating change – are essential to convert potential changes into reality. These strategies gather into three pools of consideration:

(1) Strategies to overcome resistance

(2) Strategies to unfreeze an organization

(3) Strategies for participation

Of these three topics, resistance was dealt with in the preceding chapter. This chapter moves to the second consideration, that of unfreezing organizations. Then, Part III describes strategies for participation.

## UNFREEZING

As noted earlier, unfreezing is the most difficult phase of change. How do I get someone who is comfortable with the status quo to move forward to new possibilities? How do I motivate people to change?

The answer is simple. I must manage their strain, potency, and valence (Frohman, 1970). These are the keys to motivating change. Changees who feel pressure or a need to change (strain), who have a profound sense that change can be accomplished (potency), and who believe the change promises something for them personally (valence, or payoff) will indeed change. But all three conditions must be present. Diagnosing these conditions accurately and then addressing each appropriately must form the core of your strategies for change.

## STRATEGIES FOR STRAIN

Comfort is the enemy of change. People will not change unless they experience discomfort or a need to change. But what if the changees are comfortable where they are? What can be done? Devore (1994), in researching this issue, found five categories of positive, stress-inducing strategies:

(1) Authoritative command
(2) Sanctions
(3) Evaluation
(4) Targeting
(5) Norm incongruence

### Authoritative Command

Stress can be created by imposing change through rule of authority, or position power. Our life experiences are filled with such stressors. I remember the first time I asked my parents for permission to go to a friend's house far away and they said no. I asked why, and they responded with the proverbial, "Because we said so." To them, there need be no better reason; they were the parents, and I was the child.

Authority can create stress that drives people toward change. But that stress lasts only as long as direct pressure can be maintained. Authoritative command also has much "get even" built into it (Folk Wisdom 6) and, when used repeatedly, creates organizational toxicity. As a producer of stress for positive change, this strategy can work and many bosses use it, but it has too many secondary negative consequences for a primary strategy in the long term.

In the 1990s effective managers should avoid acting "the boss," ruling by dint of position, because the zone of authority acceptance is narrower than in previous times. People expect to be treated with respect; they fight authoritative commands. The resulting conflict may be productive in inducing the strain necessary for change, but the strategy should be used in only the most entrenched situations.

### Sanctions

Jellison (1993) refers to sanctions as the "if not . . . then . . ." strategy. Sanctions involve either withholding from someone something they like or doing something to them that hurts.

Let me illustrate with dieting. I had a colleague, an ardent feminist, who wanted to lose twenty pounds. She promised herself a $500 shopping spree at Nordstrom's if she did it. But we know that positive rewards are not enough; most people do not reach their goals without stress to do so. In this case, she and I agreed on an appropriate sanction. If she did not lose the twenty pounds by Labor Day, then I would send a $500 check of hers (already written) to the Jesse Helms reelection campaign. As an ardent feminist and equally ardent liberal, she would have suffered great pain from this act. She lost the twenty pounds and never had to send the money.

I had another case, a client who wanted to be less sarcastic with his employees, so we established the following sanction for him. For every put-down statement that his secretary heard him make to an employee, she earned one extra hour of vacation. Over the span of six weeks, she acquired forty-plus hours of extra time off. Part of our sanction agreement was that he could not replace her during that extra time. While she was gone, his life was hell as he tried to handle correspondence, phones, and the like. But after that experience, he became very careful about put-downs. He had something valuable to lose and, therefore, was under pressure to change.

Sanctions can lead to discomfort, and discomfort is often a primary precondition for unfreezing. Sanctions only work, however, either if you have the power to impose them or if both parties share a mutual willingness to adopt them.

## Evaluation

A fundamental adage in the literature on evaluation is "The behavior you get is the behavior you measure." I once had a client who wanted his Vice-President for Sales to include his staff in decision making. The CEO complained that he had talked and talked to Fred, but without success. I asked whether he included this variable in his yearly formal evaluation. The CEO looked at me as if I were an alien presence. "Well, no . . ." he said. It had never occurred to him that evaluation might be used as a stress-inducing strategy and that when he failed to measure inclusive behavior, he also failed to cause it to occur. The mere suggestion of evaluation raises stress, regardless of the message.

When I know I am being watched and assessed, my behavior tends strongly toward the behaviors that are desired. This is a formalized version of the Hawthorne Effect.

### Targeting

Targeting is a wolf-in-sheep's-clothing strategy. I had an elementary school where the administration wanted all staff to use a hands-on approach to teaching science. One of the best teachers was most resistant to the change, so we targeted her. We asked her to present at the upcoming staff meeting some of her ideas about making hands-on science work. She demurred, saying "I'm not sure it will work." I replied, "Give us your best insight and cautions and then maybe lead a discussion." Every time I saw her after that, I asked, "How's the presentation coming? I'm looking forward to your insights." These comments were always positive, but they kept the pressure up.

This is using attention as Chinese water torture. You maintain stress for positive change through recurrent and positive attention to desired behavior and the changee's manifestation of that behavior.

### Norm Incongruence

Norm incongruence is the most benign of the stressors. With this strategy you tell the changees about something occurring elsewhere or you send people to visit other effective operations. You make them aware how "out of round" they are in comparison with other sites or individuals. When individuals or groups feel they are behind others — passé, ineffective, outmoded, or the like — they create pressure within themselves to get out ahead, or at least in the running with everyone else. You often see this phenomenon with technological advances. People manifest an urge to be state-of-the-art. Total Quality Management (TQM) has spread rapidly for this same reason — organizations copy new approaches so as not to be outmoded.

Norm incongruence, unfortunately, is also the drive behind the propagation of many fads. Good leaders must differentiate between needed changes and fads.

Norm incongruence is the least toxic of the stress inducers because it leaves the individual to accept, or reject, the challenge of becoming a bellwether rather than a follower. But because it is benign, it can also be the least effective.

### *Choose the Strategy for the Situation*

The five stress-inducing strategies for positive change have been presented in order of severity: authoritative command is the harshest, with the greatest negative secondary effects, while norm incongruence is the gentlest but has the greatest chance for failure. The change strategist must determine (1) the degree of ingrained comfort in the status quo, and (2) the degree to which each strategy is available to the change agent. If the changer has no position power, authoritative command is not available. On the other hand, in the face of a change that is only mildly uncomfortable, sanctions create more stress than necessary and targeting may be strong enough. Choose the strategy befitting the situation.

### STRATEGIES FOR POTENCY

Potency is a technical term in organizational theory; it means belief in one's ability to change. This was talked about earlier in Chapter 2. To achieve change, you must believe in your capacity to change. If you believe you can't fight city hall, then indeed you won't. The belief becomes a self-fulfilling prophecy. Basically, only three strategies are available for increasing potency: baby steps, wins, and paradigm breakdowns.

### *Baby Steps*

When you wanted your child to walk, you encouraged small baby steps. Humans learn any behavior in the same fashion—one step at a time. How large a stride the changer can take makes no difference; all that matters is the size of the step of the changee.

I remember the first time I learned to use a menu-driven computer program. A friend who was truly an expert tried to teach me. "All you need do is this and this and this and this and this and this and this and . . ." I was so confused, I was lucky if I could remember how to turn the machine on. A far less expert friend sat me down and had me find the menu. We experimented for a while until I could do it with reasonable facility. Then I tried to do one word-processing function— just one. Eventually, I learned the whole system, but only through baby steps. You cannot create change all at once. It comes through successive approximations of mastery.

Let me give you a corporate example of baby steps. I was working with a company that wanted to shift from manually recording phone orders to inputting them directly into a computer. The operators each took about forty orders a day. They strongly resisted the change; they wanted to input the orders as a separate step later in the day. "We can't talk to the customer and use the compter at the same time," they insisted. What would you have told the boss to do?

It was suggested that Vince, the CEO, start the first week by giving each operator thirty-five manual order forms per day. Each operator would then need to enter about five orders daily directly into the computer. The second week he reduced the manual forms to thirty; by week three they were at twenty; by week four, at ten. Thus, we made the shift over the span of five weeks simply by taking baby steps. They were probably capable of making the change in less time, except that they did not believe it could work. When the change was broken down into smaller units, the changees could develop belief in themselves.

### Wins

Critical to change is success. If you experience failure, you will avoid change; but if you achieve success, you will want to do it again. When you break a change down into its smaller subunits, be sure to celebrate the success of each step along the way. As your child makes his first faltering step forward, you do not chide him. You do not say, "Hurry up! You can do better!" No, you lavish praise and hugs. You celebrate success.

I knew a superintendent who wanted site-based management at all her schools. But no one moved fast enough to suit her, and no step was celebrated. "It's their job. I'll celebrate when they get it done," she declared. She never did see anyone running with the change, and she soon left the district, frustrated. They had not failed; she had. She failed to recognize the theory of small wins and its importance in shifting a culture.

### Experiencing Paradigm Breakdowns

In 1954, Roger Bannister accomplished an impossible feat—he broke the barrier of the four-minute mile. Theorists had long agreed that the human body would fall apart before it could experience a three-minute fifty-nine-second mile. When Bannister did it, he shocked the world.

Yet other runners soon followed suit. When the impossible becomes possible, when accepted paradigms break down, people begin believing in themselves, in their capacity for change.

Joel Barker (1992) tells the interesting tale of the Swiss watchmaker who invented the digital watch. No Swiss manufacturer would buy the innovation because it had no moving parts. It "wasn't a watch." The Japanese, on the other hand, believed in the digital innovation and soon became the leading manufacturer of timepieces.

When paradigms shatter, they open the floodgates for change. One of the realities that Fullan (1994) describes is the effect of breaking paradigms on creating whole new possibilities for change. Probably, most of us will not be in the business of fundamental paradigm shifts, but we will be involved in shattering a lot of little paradigms. Even at this microlevel, shifting paradigms is important in creating potency.

## STRATEGIES FOR VALENCE

Valence translates simply to payoffs: What is in it for the changees? People do not change unless they see some clear and positive payoff for themselves. Each of us is different, and each of us must be examined individually; nevertheless, we can identify some general classes of payoffs. Herzberg (1959) and his progeny theorists suggest the following taxonomy:

- recognition
- responsibility
- achievement
- money/resources
- interpersonal relations
- facilities
- security

Jellison (1993) suggests other, more concrete, examples of payoffs:

- special rules
- scheduling adjustments
- altered work assignments
- independence
- education support
- perks

- coalition
- space and equipment
- information
- promotions
- praise
- informal benefits
- third party trades
- money, etc.

Whatever lens you use to assess payoffs (I generally use the Herzberg categories), be aware that appropriate payoffs for the changees are critical to success.

You should not examine your payoffs but those of the changees. They are the ones attempting to change. The best way to make this assessment is to ask people "What would need to be in this change for you to get you to do it? What would be your payoff?"

Do not allude to some vast principle like "This would be good for the kids" or "This would help the company grow." Be specific, be clear, and orient yourself to the changee.

## CRAFTING THE OVERALL STRATEGY

Four steps must be taken to craft an overall strategy for change:

(1) Diagnose strain, potency, and valence of the changee.
(2) Determine deficit conditions.
(3) Match strategies to individuals and deficits.
(4) Blend strategy elements together.

### Diagnosis

The first step is to assess the degree of strain, potency, and valence the changees are experiencing. These factors are the keys to unfreezing. Rest assured that one or more of them must be absent; otherwise unfreezing would already have occurred. The change would already have begun.

### Deficit Conditions

The second step is to determine which of the three conditions needs to be addressed. You can ignore those conditions that are present and focus on the missing elements.

## *Matching Strategies*

The third step is to match strategies to the deficit. For instance, if potency and valence are present, but strain is not, then your best strategy would encompass increased discomfort. For this, you might want to use evaluation or targeting approaches.

## *Blended Elements*

When all the elements of your strategy have been identified, they may overlap. You will need to blend them together into a single, overall strategy. Remember, too, to harmonize your unfreezing strategies with those you identified to address resistance. You are now ready for Part II – Performing Change.

# PERFORMING CHANGE

# CHAPTER 5

# Change Checklist

CHANGE is a complex process that must be managed simply or it eludes us. This chapter presents a twenty-step checklist for creating change in individuals and organizations; the checklist builds on ideas and concepts already presented in Part I. You may want to add your own steps or elements to this checklist.

These twenty steps, validated by England (1992), pass through the stages of analysis (steps 1–8), planning (steps 9–15), and implementation and evaluation (steps 16–20). Figure 5.1 summarizes the steps.

In proposing these steps, I make an assumption that will be explained more fully in Chapter 8. The assumption is that change is best accomplished through teams. Change can be brought about by an individual, but usually with less satisfaction and less success. Therefore, I assume that you are working with a group of people with similar, but occasionally conflicting, interests who have come together as a team to improve the functioning of the organization. Whether performed by an individual or a team, however, the steps are the same.

Let me turn to an explanation of each step and then end the chapter with the forms that make up the Change Checklist.

**Analysis**
1. Description
2. Need
3. Potential actors
4. Payoff
5. Unfreezing
6. Resistance
7 Investment
8. Culture

**Planning**
9. Actual changees
10 Change strategy
11. Resistance strategy
12. Participation
13 Excitement
14. Change environment
15. Scope

**Implementation and Evaluation**
16. Advocates
17. Time frame
18. Monitoring
19. Action plans
20. Risk analysis

*Figure 5.1.  Steps in the change process.*

```
┌─────────────────────────────────┐
│       ANALYSIS                  │
│  →    Description               │
│       Need                      │
│       Potential Actors          │
│       Payoff                    │
│       Unfreezing                │
│       Resistance                │
│       Investment                │
│       Culture                   │
└─────────────────────────────────┘
```

## ANALYSIS

### *Description*

The first stage of change is analysis, and the first step of analysis is description. Description looks at two fundamental issues: (1) the change itself and (2) clarity of expression. Just as in problem solving, where the most critical step is to define the problem, so must a change--what you want--be stated precisely and clearly. Too often change efforts fail because members of a group have different presumptions about what they want to accomplish.

If the change is not described in one short paragraph using simple English, then it is not clear enough. Do not assume that everyone knows what you mean; usually they do not. Therefore, the first step in the Change Checklist is to describe the change effort in one short, clear paragraph.

Each step will be followed with an example to show how the checklist works. Forms to lead you through the entire process appear at the end of this chapter. Figure 5.2 begins a series of examples to show how the forms might be used.

---

**Communication and Literacy Program (CLP)**

Describe the intended change in one paragraph:

This change effort intends to create a program of training over the next two years that:

- Remediates the reading and writing skills of employees
- Improves the oral presentation skills of managers
- Improves the written communication skills of managers

---

*Figure 5.2. Sample description of intended change (Form 1).*

```
┌────────────────────────────────┐
│       ANALYSIS                 │
│         Description            │
│   →     Need                   │
│         Potential Actors       │
│         Payoff                 │
│         Unfreezing             │
│         Resistance             │
│         Investment             │
│         Culture                │
└────────────────────────────────┘
```

## *Need*

With a description in hand, we turn to need. A wonderful old adage strikes at the heart of this problem: "If it ain't broke, don't fix it!" We have all seen a new CEO, associate superintendent, or project manager who wants to make a name for himself very quickly. So he lists seventeen items in the organization that need to be changed immediately. He takes little time to diagnose the setting. He may need change but the organization does not, and we all know the disastrous results.

You must be sure that a need for change exists in the organization and is recognized by its members. Is there really a need for this program/proposal? Can you show that need clearly? Do not take these questions lightly. Many so-called reforms could have been avoided and resources saved if someone had been more tough-minded about posing such questions. Enough fundamental and necessary changes are needed so that inventing unnecessary changes is itself unnecessary.

The second step of the checklist brings you face to face with this issue. Step 2 asks you to describe the need for change in a paragraph or two (see Figure 5.3 and Form 1 at the end of this chapter).

| **Statement of Need** | **CLP Project** |

What facts show the need for this change?

1. Thirteen percent of workers have limited English-speaking skills.
2. Over 28% of workers have little English writing ability.
3. Thirty-four percent of a random sample of memos written by managers were judged below acceptable writing standards by outside experts.
4. Middle and upper managers have requested help in oral presentation skills; they feel inadequate in front of groups.

*Figure 5.3. Sample statement of need (Form 1).*

```
┌─────────────────────────────────┐
│      ANALYSIS                    │
│        Description               │
│        Need                      │
│   →    Potential Actors          │
│        Payoff                    │
│        Unfreezing                │
│        Resistance                │
│        Investment                │
│        Culture                   │
└─────────────────────────────────┘
```

## Potential Actors

To reflect on the people involved in a change effort is another step often overlooked. Who are the changers? Which individuals stand behind the change—want it to happen? These folks come quickly to mind. Less obvious, and far more important at this stage, are the potential changees. Who are the people you must influence to create the desired change? Remember, changees differ in their reasons for resisting. Therefore, you must understand the changees and their needs.

For step 3, you and your team list the names of potential changees (see Figure 5.4 and Form 2). Name names, for in so doing you identify differences in perceptions among changees and also personalize potential resisters. At this stage of the change process, both sets of information place you at an advantage. Do you find you have too many people to name? If so, then the change may be too big (break it down into smaller steps—or rethink your list for greater precision). In either case, identifying potential actors serves as a reality check.

| POTENTIAL CHANGEES | | CLP PROJECT |
|---|---|---|
| **Name** | **Position** | **Reason for Listing as Potential Changee** |
| 7 maintenance workers (Angela, Brad, Tom S., Barzy, Manuel, Sheila, Tom R.) | Maintenance | Poor literacy skills |
| 6 food service staff | Cooks and servers | Poor literacy skills |
| John Jones | Middle manager | Requested help in oral presentation; needs writing skills |
| Bill Smith | Middle manager | Requested help in oral presentation; needs writing skills |
| Harry Chin | Middle manager | Requested help in oral presentation; needs writing skills |
| Maria Flores | Middle manager | Requested help in oral presentation |
| Jim Walsh | Assistant CEO | Requested help with oral presentation |
| Tim Morrison | CEO | Needs top brass support |

*Figure 5.4.* Sample list of potential changees (Form 2).

```
┌─────────────────────────────────┐
│    ANALYSIS                      │
│      Description                 │
│      Need                        │
│      Potential Actors            │
│  →   Payoff                      │
│      Unfreezing                  │
│      Resistance                  │
│      Investment                  │
│      Culture                     │
└─────────────────────────────────┘
```

## *Payoff*

What's in it for the changee? What will he or she gain from the change effort? As stated repeatedly, this may be the single most important question you ask. Look at payoff as positive, necessary, and sane. Without payoff, people should not willingly change. Change under those circumstances makes no sense.

A school district that wanted to create a teacher advisory program illustrates this point nicely. In the proposed program, teachers would spend their free periods counseling a small group of students. The district asked me for help, and I, in turn, asked them about payoff— "What's in it for the teachers?"

"It'll ease up the registration process and gain counselors a lot more time," was their reply.

Great! I asked, "What's in it for teachers?"

"The counselors can use their extra time to help administer the school," they replied.

Great! "What's in it for the teachers?" I queried one last time.

"It will be really good for the students," came the final appeal.

Somehow they could not grasp the issue of payoff for the changees, the teachers—they concentrated only on the benefits for everyone else. And guess what? The program never succeeded.

If you seek success in your change efforts, you must examine the benefits—not to yourself, but to the changee. Remember Folk Wisdom 2—Not Everyone is Like Me. If I fail to uncover her need or his payoff, and link my change to it, I radically decrease my chance of success. So step 4 in the Change Checklist is to list the changees and the benefits to each of them (see Figure 5.5 and Form 3).

| PAYOFF ANALYSIS | CLP PROJECT |
|---|---|
| **Name of Changee** | **Potential Payoffs** |
| Maintenance workers | Promotability |
| Food service workers | Better self-concept |
| | At-home skills |
| Jones, Smith, Chin | Promotability |
| | Improved performance appraisals in area of written communication |
| | More comfort with speeches to board and clients |
| Flores, Walsh | More comfort with speeches to board and public; better press relations |
| Morrison | Better relations with staff |
| | Seen as "regular guy" |
| | Better writing skills |

*Figure 5.5. Sample payoff analysis (Form 3).*

```
ANALYSIS
   Description
   Need
   Potential Actors
   Payoff
→  Unfreezing
   Resistance
   Investment
   Culture
```

## Unfreezing

The importance of Lewin's (1951) and Frohman's (1970) conception of change was discussed earlier. The three powerful preconditions for unfreezing people, for getting them off the dime, are strain, valence, and potency.

(1) Strain — Do the individuals feel stress in relation to change, or a problem linked to the change? No stress, no change. Too much stress, no change. Eustress is necessary. What is the level of the *changee's* stress (not yours)?

(2) Valence — Is there something valuable to head towards? Is point B a positive that lures you forward, rather than simply a neutral alternative to negative point A? This attraction of point B is the concrete manifestation of payoff. As noted in Chapter 2, if you lack a clear vision of your objective, then you will most assuredly not leave where you are. Point B must be clear, positive, and valuable to the changee.

(3) Potency — Does the changee believe he can change? If not, then indeed he will not change. The question is: How does he perceive the possibility of success? Whether or not this perception is well founded is of no importance. Potency deals with belief, not facts. People who believe they can change have the potential to do so. Conversely and more powerfully, those who believe they cannot change, cannot and will not.

The fifth step in the Change Checklist is an analysis of readiness for unfreezing (see Figure 5.6 and Form 4). Consider each change for strain, valence, and potency.

| Name of Changee | READINESS FOR UNFREEZING Appropriate Strain? | Positive Valence? | CLP PROJECT Adequate Potency? |
|---|---|---|---|
| Maintenance workers | Yes | Yes | No |
| Food service workers (except Estella) | No | No | No |
| Estella | Yes | Yes | No |
| Jones | Yes | Yes | Yes |
| Smith | Yes | Yes | No |
| Chin | Yes | Yes | Yes |
| Flores | No | Yes | Yes |
| Walsh | No | Yes | Yes |
| Morrison | No | Yes | Yes |

*Strain.* Problem for food service workers, Flores, Walsh, and Morrison. Need more strain before they will do much.

*Valence* Not a major problem except for the six food service workers; need to be shown value of the program. Everyone else has bought in.

*Potency* Not a problem for managers except Smith, but a problem for workers. Need to be convinced they can change in these areas.

*Figure 5.6. Sample unfreezing analysis (Form 4).*

```
┌─────────────────────────────┐
│      ANALYSIS               │
│        Description          │
│        Need                 │
│        Potential Actors     │
│        Payoff               │
│        Unfreezing           │
│   →    Resistance           │
│        Investment           │
│        Culture              │
└─────────────────────────────┘
```

## *Resistance*

An entire chapter addressed this subject by discussing fifteen potential sources of resistance to change. To what degree are these sources evident in your change effort? Do you find other additional sources idiosyncratic to your setting? Are some factors applicable to certain changees but not others? Resistance interacts with payoff and unfreezing to give the change strategist a sound understanding of the changees. From this understanding, the changer designs interventions to reduce resistance.

Obviously, the less the resistance, the higher your probability of success. Therefore, the sixth step in the Change Checklist is to evaluate sources of resistance to change (see Figure 5.7 and Form 5).

| POTENTIAL RESISTANCE FACTORS | | | | | CLP PROJECT |
| --- | --- | --- | --- | --- | --- |
| **In this change effort, to what extent do you find:** | **Not at all** | | | | **Very much so** |
| Lack of ownership | 1 | 2 | ③ | 4 | 5 |
| Lack of benefits | 1 | ② | 3 | 4 | 5 |
| Increased burdens | 1 | 2 | 3 | 4 | ⑤ |
| Lack of top brass support | ① | 2 | 3 | 4 | 5 |
| Loneliness | 1 | ② | 3 | 4 | 5 |
| Insecurity | 1 | ② | 3 | 4 | 5 |
| Norm incongruence | 1 | ② | 3 | 4 | 5 |
| Boredom | 1 | 2 | 3 | ④ | 5 |
| Chaos | 1 | ② | 3 | 4 | 5 |
| Superiority | 1 | ② | 3 | 4 | 5 |
| Differential knowledge | 1 | ② | 3 | 4 | 5 |
| Lack of recognition | 1 | ② | 3 | 4 | 5 |
| Sudden, wholesale change | 1 | ② | 3 | 4 | 5 |
| Failure | 1 | 2 | 3 | ④ | 5 |
| Extremes of organizational structure | 1 | ② | 3 | 4 | 5 |
| Unique sources | 1 | 2 | 3 | 4 | 5 |

*Figure 5.7. Sample resistance rating (Form 5).*

```
┌─────────────────────────────────┐
│           ANALYSIS              │
│           Description           │
│           Need                  │
│           Potential Actors      │
│           Payoff                │
│           Unfreezing            │
│           Resistance            │
│      →    Investment            │
│           Culture               │
└─────────────────────────────────┘
```

## *Investment*

You have already identified the changers, but who else already supports the change? Recognizing supporters is useful for three reasons.
First of all, you will save the time often spent convincing those who are
already convinced. Classic decision theory identifies three general
audiences: (1) those who already support your position, (2) those
against it, and (3) those undecided. In trying to effect a decision, one
need not worry about groups one and two. You have little likelihood of
driving away supporters or converting opponents. To gear change
strategies to the group that already agrees is a waste of energy and
time. Group two may just possibly be retrievable. But certainly group
three should be the focus of attention.

A second reason for knowing your supporters is equally important.
Your supporters often get behind you, push the change, and increase
the drivers. They demand and push and argue and sell and push. In
Chapter 3, you read that to increase pushing, or drivers, is not the most
effective approach to change. Sometimes true believers inadvertently
become the worst enemies of change. The more these true believers
push, the more they increase resistance and opposition. Sometimes you
need to calm down your supporters, to temper their approach.

Lastly, although supporters are inappropriate objects for change
strategies, they require attention of another kind; they require support
and reassurance.

Step 7 in the Change Checklist asks that you list your supporters,
those folks who have already invested themselves in the change (Figure
5.8 and Form 6). Reinforce your supporters. Include them as partners
in the process. A little recognition goes a long way.

| LIST OF SUPPORTERS | | CLP PROJECT |
|---|---|---|
| **Name** | **Reason for Listing as Supporter** | |
| 1. Board | Has already approved program. | |
| 2. CEO | Actively supported recommendation to board; sees as jumping-off point to quality circles. | |

*Figure 5.8.  Sample list of supporters (Form 6).*

> ANALYSIS
> Description
> Need
> Potential Actors
> Payoff
> Unfreezing
> Resistance
> Investment
> → Culture

## *Culture*

Does the organizational culture support change? Several available instruments assess organizational and individual readiness for change (e.g., Jones and Bearley, 1986; Pfeiffer and Jones, 1978). All of them recognize that change is easier or more difficult depending on the organization's cultural inclination toward innovation and risk. The stronger the change culture, the bolder the potential change. Do the top brass support change? Is the organizational structure conducive to change? Has the organization experienced a history of successful change? These questions examine relevant aspects of culture. Therefore, the eighth step of the Change Checklist involves describing the organization's culture for change (Figure 5.9 and Form 6).

> **Culture for Change**        **CLP Project**
>
> This organization has repeatedly experienced new programs with fairly good success. There is a new CEO, and employees are a little unsure of his intentions. He seems to be a mover and shaker. This is a small organization with a positive culture toward change.

*Figure 5.9. Sample description of culture for change (Form 6).*

```
┌─────────────────────────────────────┐
│        PLANNING                      │
│   →    Actual Changees               │
│        Change Strategy               │
│        Resistance Strategy           │
│        Participation                 │
│        Excitement                    │
│        Change Environment            │
│        Scope                         │
└─────────────────────────────────────┘
```

## PLANNING

### *Actual Changees*

The previous eight steps dealt with analysis. Next, the Change Checklist moves into planning.

You identified the list of potential changees in step 3. Now is the time to delimit the list to the actual changees. To do this, it is important to use these criteria to evaluate your potential pool:

(1) How influential is each of those individuals as an actor in your organization?

(2) How much do they need to change?

(3) How feasible is it to change each of these potential changees?

The ninth step in the Change Checklist is to select actual changees by assessing their influence in the organization, their need for change, and the degree to which each is changeable (see Figure 5.10 and Form 7). In assessing the list of potential changees, the first two criteria are clearly the most important. If the key question is, Whom do I need to change to be successful? then influence and need are the dominant issues. Most often however, we think first of feasibility—who is easiest to change—and let that color our selection of actual changees. To counter that tendency, the range of the rating scales for influence and need in Form 7 is greater than that for changeability. Influence and need should be the dominant issues.

| | ACTUAL CHANGEES | | | CLP PROJECT |
|---|---|---|---|---|
| **Name of Potential Changee** | **Influence Low→High (1–9)** | **Need Low→High (1–9)** | **Changeability Low→High (1–5)** | **Total** |
| 1. Maintenance workers | 4 | 8 | 4 | 16 |
| 2. Food service workers | 4 | 8 | 2 | 14 |
| 3. Estella | 6 | 6 | 5 | 17 |
| 4. Jones | 4 | 6 | 5 | 15 |
| 5. Smith | 4 | 6 | 4 | 14 |
| 6. Chin | 4 | 6 | 5 | 15 |
| 7. Flores | 5 | 3 | 2 | 10 |
| 8. Walsh | 7 | 4 | 4 | 15 |
| 9. Morrison | 9 | 2 | 2 | 13 |

*Figure 5.10. Sample list of actual changees (Form 7).*

```
┌─────────────────────────────────────┐
│     PLANNING                         │
│        Actual Changees               │
│  →     Change Strategy               │
│        Resistance Strategy           │
│        Participation                 │
│        Excitement                    │
│        Change Environment            │
│        Scope                         │
└─────────────────────────────────────┘
```

## Change Strategy

Using the Chin and Benne framework (1985), what will be your change strategy—rational-empirical, power-coercive, or normative-reeducative? You may know that the organization is fundamentally rational, susceptible to data/knowledge strategies. If so, choose a rational-empirical approach. This approach calls for integration of data and logical analysis.

Or you may realize that time is of the essence and that the institution is so frozen that stress is needed. In that case, choose a power-coercive approach, recognizing the negatives fundamental to such an approach (see Chapter 2).

Or you may be interested in long-term change and wish to link the change with people's needs and drives. Then, choose a normative-reeducative strategy. This last approach is the one chosen by most planned-change strategists.

But seldom does one use a single, pure approach. Most often, successful change is a function of a sensitive combination of these three strategy types. For example,

(1) Affirmative action was initially a power-coercive strategy (Executive Order 11246) followed by slow, long-term understanding of the fundamental importance of equity (combining normative-reeducative and rational-empirical strategies).
(2) Many substance abuse programs are built on linking individual drives (positive and negative) with the substance being abused. This normative-reeducative process is supported by periodic injections of guilt (power-coercive strategy).
(3) The Peters and Austin (1985) strategy of Management By Walking

Around (MBWA) is effective because it satisfies employee needs to be heard and to associate with superiors (normative-reeducative strategy), while also providing useful information to the leader (rational-empirical strategy).

At this point, you construct your strategies, as described in Chapter 4. Having already completed your diagnosis in step 5, you now add the other elements from this section to begin an overall strategy of change. The Strategy Sheet, Form 8, reminds you to identify strategies in this, the tenth, step in the Change Checklist (see example in Figure 5.11).

---

**CHANGE STRATEGY**              **CLP PROJECT**

RE = rational—empirical
PC = power—coercive
NR = normative—reeducative

Morrison has low need for change; must target his leadership need, his desire to be seen as a change agent. We need his participation, but need not change him personally.

Food service workers are biggest challenge. Need to create strain by making communication part of performance appraisal; link inservice with salary. Must find payoffs for them and convince them they can change. Start small to build potency (theory of small wins).

Estella needs support; eager to change but not sure of herself; needs success experiences (NR). Same is true of Smith and maintenance workers (NR).

Chin needs no change.
Smith and Walsh are . . .

---

*Figure 5.11. Sample change strategy (Form 8).*

```
┌─────────────────────────────────┐
│   PLANNING                      │
│     Actual Changees             │
│     Change Strategy             │
│  →  Resistance Strategy         │
│     Participation               │
│     Excitement                  │
│     Change Environment          │
│     Scope                       │
└─────────────────────────────────┘
```

## Resistance Strategy

In step 6 you assessed various sources of resistance to change. Which of these will you address in your change plan? You need to select a response to each of the high-scoring resistance factors. There is nothing technical about the actions. They come out of logic, experience, and horse sense. Which actions overcome the sources of resistance identified? For step 11 of the Change Checklist, use your team to brainstorm responses to resistance (see Figure 5.12 and Form 8).

| RESISTANCE STRATEGY | CLP PROJECT |
|---|---|
| **High-Scoring Sources of Resistance (see Form 5)** | **Responses** |
| Increased burdens (time) | All employees must realize that they will have released time or reduced duties to compensate for in-service time. |
| Boredom | Present early efforts in a festive manner. Emphasize fun! |
| Failure | Take change in baby steps, not too much at once. Start with easier literacy skills and build up. |

*Figure 5.12. Sample resistance strategy (Form 8).*

```
┌─────────────────────────────────────┐
│     PLANNING                         │
│        Actual Changees               │
│        Change Strategy               │
│        Resistance Strategy           │
│    →   Participation                 │
│        Excitement                    │
│        Change Environment            │
│        Scope                         │
└─────────────────────────────────────┘
```

## *Participation*

Earlier, in step 7, you identified the supporters of the change effort. At that point we discussed the importance of investment in the project. The single best predictor of such investment is participation, or involvement. How do you plan to involve changees in the process? Will they participate both in defining the desired change and in planning for implementation? Remember, involvement is richer if changees are involved in both phases, but at times, the definition comes ready-made. If changees cannot help form the vision, then they must participate in crafting its implementation. This twelfth step asks you to identify how changees will be involved (see Figure 5.13 and Form 9).

```
┌─────────────────────────────────────────────────────────┐
│          PARTICIPATION               CLP PROJECT         │
│ • Have managers define prizes or payoffs for communication│
│   growth. Do the same for workers.                       │
│ • Have both groups define work with trainer to diagnose   │
│   starting levels.                                       │
└─────────────────────────────────────────────────────────┘
```

*Figure 5.13. Sample participation plan (Form 9).*

| PLANNING |
| :--- |
| Actual Changees |
| Change Strategy |
| Resistance Strategy |
| Participation |
| → Excitement |
| Change Environment |
| Scope |

## *Excitement*

How will you create excitement for the change? Where's the party? Bandwagons are created when someone orchestrates the energy and zeal aroused by a change effort. We often labor under the misapprehension that change calls for somber and grave tones. The opposite is true. The more important the change, the more fun and excitement it must generate!

Commitment and participation grow out of association with something spirited and enjoyable. Dedicated alumni talk not about the painful process of writing papers and exams, but about the excitement of sports, dances, and friends. Great speakers typically use humor and drama, not cold logic. Successful salesmen know the power of personal association and pleasurable experiences. The thirteenth step of the Change Checklist builds excitement into the change process (see Figure 5.14 and Form 9). Schedule events that are stimulating, and establish a tone that your endeavor is exciting and enjoyable.

---

**EXCITEMENT**                              **CLP PROJECT**

At step 11, fun emerged as especially important for this change. So . . .

• Have trainer design contest for workers.
• Have trainer design separate contests for managers.
• Have kickoff ice cream social.
• Provide prizes for winners.

---

*Figure 5.14. Sample excitement plan (Form 9).*

```
┌─────────────────────────────────┐
│     PLANNING                     │
│     Actual Changees              │
│     Change Strategy              │
│     Resistance Strategy          │
│     Participation                │
│     Excitement                   │
│  →  Change Environment           │
│     Scope                        │
└─────────────────────────────────┘
```

## *Change Environment*

Few changes occur in isolation. Instead, they come in clusters or sequences. You need to know how your change fits into the patterns created by other changes in the organization for four reasons:

(1) Change demands resources (money, time, energy). If numerous other changes are in progress, you may find no resources available for your effort. You may want to wait for a more propitious time.

(2) The success of your change may depend upon the success of a prior change effort as yet unfinished. You need to look for cumulative effect.

(3) Others may be depending on your success as a foundation for later changes. These people become natural allies for your effort.

(4) Your point B may require a series of smaller change efforts, leading through $A_1$, $A_2$, etc. If so, you need to determine where you fit in the overall strategic plan.

These issues call for examination of your setting. The place of your change effort in your organization's pattern of change guides you in choosing the best time and mobilizing appropriate resources and supporters. Step 14 in the Change Checklist, Form 9, reminds you to look at the change environment in your organization (see example in Figure 5.15).

**CHANGE ENVIRONMENT** **CLP PROJECT**

Where does this effort fit into the pattern of change?

The CEO is new and positively oriented toward change. He wants this one to work, and he is willing to be patient. This change is the first step in his thrust for better communication with internal and external groups. Other marketing and communication workshops will follow.

Management is accustomed to change, but workers are not. Managers are committed to training. This is a moderately high need for them.

This the first staff development for workers. When this change succeeds, other needs will be identified and pursued. This need is not critical, but it is a good starting point for workers.

***Figure 5.15.*** *Sample analysis of change environment (Form 9).*

```
┌─────────────────────────────────────┐
│     PLANNING                         │
│     Actual Changees                  │
│     Change Strategy                  │
│     Resistance Strategy              │
│     Participation                    │
│     Excitement                       │
│     Change Environment               │
│ →   Scope                            │
└─────────────────────────────────────┘
```

## Scope

The last element of the planning phase, step 15 in the Change Checklist, asks you to examine the scope of the change effort. In some cases, the proposed change may be unduly ambitious, trying to do too much at once. Since no one gains by failure, you need to scale down an oversized project to increase its probability of success. Conversely, some efforts are too trivial; they may succeed, but so what? The gain is inconsequential.

What are the criteria for judging sufficiency of scope? Let me pose the following:

(1) If implemented, will the change measurably carry forward the objectives of the organization?

(2) Do you have the resources (time, money, energy) minimally necessary to complete the effort?

(3) Can the change be accomplished in one to two years?

(4) Can the organization continue to function normally while the change effort is occurring?

If the answer is no to question one, then the project is too trivial. If the answer is no to question two, three, or four, then the scope is too broad. The decision tree, Form 10, illustrates a pathway through this issue of scope. Figure 5.16 illustrates the yes/no questions that might lead to a go/no-go decision). After completing this step, you are ready to move forward from planning to implementation and evaluation.

| SCOPE | | CLP PROJECT |
|---|---|---|
| Impact on objectives? | Yes | |
| Sufficient resources? | Yes | |
| Occur in one to two years? | Yes | |
| Organization continue to function? | Yes | |
| Decision: Implement | | |

*Figure 5.16. Sample scope analysis (follow Decision Tree on Form 10).*

> IMPLEMENTATION &
> EVALUATION
> → Advocates
> 　 Time Frame
> 　 Monitoring
> 　 Action Plans
> 　 Risk Analysis

## IMPLEMENTATION AND EVALUATION

### *Advocates*

In steps 9–15 you devised your strategy. Now it's the time to implement and evaluate your plan. To implement change, you must start with a recognized advocate. Change without advocacy is diffuse and has little hope of successful completion (Hefferlin, 1969). You need someone in the organization willing to put his or her name, time, and psyche behind the change effort. Many of us have had encouragers who said, "Why don't you try to do X? We'll be right behind you and give you silent support. We just can't have our name associated with the project at this time."

This is not advocacy—it is a prescription for disaster! An advocate can come from anywhere in the organization—top, bottom, or middle—but he or she must be willing to take a visible, assertive role. I say *individual* because group advocacy seldom works. The fact that management is behind "it," or the masses are for "it," or parents want "it" is not enough. You need to name names and clearly identify the advocates.

How many advocates do you need? I recommend not more than three, because an excess of advocates diffuses leadership. A vision of change requires focused advocacy. Step 16 of the Change Checklist, Form 11, helps you establish that focus (see the example in Figure 5.17).

---

**ADVOCATES FOR CHANGE**　　　　**CLP PROJECT**
1. Lucille Hernandez, Director of Human Resource Development
2. Tim Morrison, CEO

*Figure 5.17. Sample list of advocates (Form 11).*

```
┌─────────────────────────────┐
│  IMPLEMENTATION &           │
│  EVALUATION                 │
│     Advocates               │
│  →  Time Frame              │
│     Monitoring              │
│     Action Plans            │
│     Risk Analysis           │
└─────────────────────────────┘
```

## *Time Frame*

Time management is a critical issue in implementing change. A strong characteristic of trusted managers is the capacity to establish and maintain realistic time lines. If you promise success by Thursday, and then hem and haw on Friday because you have failed to meet your time line, you are on the path to creating distrust. Conversely, if you set realistic time lines with clear steps along the way, and if you meet your deadline, people are impressed. "She's got her act together!" A key part of the action plans coming up in step 19 is time specification—just when you will achieve each element of your plan.

One year is the most desirable time span for a change effort. Two years is workable. Anything beyond that is open to the vagaries of unanticipated variables and likely to drift off course because of delayed gratification. Changees want to see success in the near term.

The proposed time frame may run counter to much of the established literature that states it takes three to five years to fully implement any meaningful change. I do not differ with those findings. But while three years may be the time period necessary for full implementation of major changes, change efforts of substance need to be broken down into smaller units of one year or less. Change strategies spanning a year are manageable. Multiyear accomplishments, therefore, need multiple strategies—each year a new conception for proceeding toward change.

Conversely, some changes may occur in less than a year, depending on the organization and circumstances. However, the shorter the time span, the more you risk limited participation. Involvement and collaboration are time-consuming. Time is necessary for people to reinvent at least part of a wheel. Efficient change all too often is only illusory change.

What is the best time frame for your change effort? Step 17 of the Change Checklist leads you to consider this question (see Figure 5.18 and Form 11).

```
┌─────────────────────────────────────────────────────────────────┐
│                      TIME FRAME                    CLP PROJECT    │
│  When to begin?          February 1                              │
│  When to complete?       November 15                             │
│  Dates of interim reports                                        │
│  Meetings in February; training to start in March                │
│  Training officer estimates eight one-hour sessions over six weeks│
│     plus two ninety-minute parties.                              │
│  Progress reports in June and September                          │
└─────────────────────────────────────────────────────────────────┘
```

*Figure 5.18.* Sample time frame (Form 11).

```
┌─────────────────────────────────┐
│  IMPLEMENTATION &               │
│  EVALUATION                     │
│  Advocates                      │
│  Time Frame                     │
│ →  Monitoring                   │
│  Action Plans                   │
│  Risk Analysis                  │
└─────────────────────────────────┘
```

## Monitoring

Nothing works for long on automatic pilot, not even planes or boats. Similarly, change plans will falter without a system for monitoring implementation of action plans and their effectiveness in reaching the desired point B. In the arcane language of evaluation, you need to carry out formative, process, and output discrepancy analysis. If you like those terms, see Stake (1967), Scriven (1967), or Anderson (1974).

If you do not, let me suggest some elements of a monitoring system.

(1) Contract—Identify the decision maker for the change effort and contract with him or her relative to uses for and recipients of the evaluation information.

(2) Time line—Determine when reports are needed, both along the way and at the end of the effort. During the first year of implementation, consider three-month feedback periods.

(3) Criteria—Identify the criteria for determining success. Be specific and clear. Ask yourself, "How will I know when my change has achieved success?"

(4) Participants—Decide who is to be involved in the evaluation team and who will provide the richest data.

(5) Methodology—Establish a reasonable and controlled methodology for collecting data. Use the full range of methodologies (see Isaac and Michaels, 1984), rather than limiting yourself to experimental designs.

(6) Simplicity—Most of all, avoid getting hung up in complexity. Scholars and experts may love complexity and obtuseness, but that does not aid practice. In designing the evaluation and interpreting the information, remember to ask, "Will this help me make better decisions about my organization?"

There is much more to evaluation than this brief sketch indicates; you may want to explore the literature in that domain. For our purposes, suffice it to say that if you never check on your progress, you'll never know when you've arrived.

What is your radar system? Who will do what, when, and how? Step 18 of the Change Checklist, Form 11, addresses this issue (see Figure 5.19 for an example).

| MONITORING SYSTEMS | CLP PROJECT |
|---|---|
| **How Will the Change Be Monitored?** | **By Whom?** |
| Outcome measures to show changes in communication skills; pretest in February; posttest in November | Trainers |
| Satisfaction surveys at the end of third and seventh inservice hours | Trainers |
| *Note: Programs may be altered on the basis of the results of these mid-course reviews.* | |
| Written summary report | Written by trainer; reviewed in draft with Hernandez and Morrison; distributed by trainer |

*Figure 5.19. Sample monitoring system (Form 11).*

```
┌─────────────────────────────────┐
│  IMPLEMENTATION &               │
│  EVALUATION                     │
│  Advocates                      │
│  Time Frame                     │
│  Monitoring                     │
│  →    Action Plans              │
│       Risk Analysis             │
└─────────────────────────────────┘
```

*Action Plans*

Action plans are blueprints for implementing change. They specify the order of actions to be taken, who is to be involved, and when each action is to occur. Form 12 at the end of this chapter provides one format for an action plan.

Jones (1972) provides five criteria for judging the adequacy of your action plan. He calls these criteria the SPIRO model.

- specificity—Is the action precise and specific?
- performance—What do you intend to accomplish?
- involvement—Who is part of the action?
- realism—Do you have the resources to do it?
- observability—Will you be able to measure/see results?

Action plans that satisfy these criteria give precise steps to change. Step 19 of the Change Checklist asks you to turn the strategies developed in steps 10–13 into a series of specific actions to take you from point A to point B. Figure 5.20 illustrates use of Form 12 to complete the action plan.

| | | ACTION PLAN | | CLP PROJECT |
|---|---|---|---|---|
| Number | Action Step | Who Is Involved? | Resources Needed | When |
| 1. | Get Morrison commitment | Hernandez– Morrison | Lunch | January 15 |
| 2. | Hire trainer | Hernandez– Morrison | $3,500 contract | February 3 |
| 3. | Trainer– Morrison confer | Morrison– trainer– Hernandez | Lunch | February 3 |
| 4. | Trainer drafts program/ trainer drafts contests | Trainer | $1,000 budget | February 4–21 |
| 5. | Hernandez drafts new performance appraisal system, including literacy requirement | Hernandez | $300 legal consultant | February 4–21 |
| 6. | Trainer– Hernandez meet with managers at ice cream party to explain program | Trainer– Hernandez– all managers | $75 | February 25 |
| 7. | Trainer– Hernandez discuss program intervention level and prizes with managers | Trainer– Hernandez– all managers | | February 25 |

*Figure 5.20.* Sample action plan (Form 12).

| ACTION PLAN | | | | CLP PROJECT |
|---|---|---|---|---|
| Number | Action Step | Who Is Involved? | Resources Needed | When |
| 8. | Trainer– Hernandez meet with workers to explain program and performance appraisal system at second ice cream party | Trainer– Hernandez– food service staff– mainte- nance staff | $200 | March 2 |
| 9. | Etc. | | | |

*Figure 5.20 (continued). Sample action plan (Form 12).*

---

IMPLEMENTATION &
EVALUATION
Advocates
Time Frame
Monitoring
Action Plans
→    Risk Analysis

---

*Risk Analysis*

Every changer quickly alerts us to the wondrous advantages of change. Advantages are important, but equally important are negative consequences of the proposed change. Remember, every change involves loss. You need to be aware of negative consequences – some small, some great. To attend only to positive consequences is to miss the array of problems associated with innovation. Computer programming is a domain of precision, expertise, and algorithms, but have you ever implemented a new software package and not had problems? If computer programming is fraught with glitches and negatives, how much more problematic must be all the changes in areas that lack precision, expertise, and algorithms. Loss and negative consequences are realities of change; unplanned for, they cause its demise.

In examining these positive and negative consequences, you need to weigh one set against the other. If the gains ( + ) of change outweigh the losses ( − ), you should proceed further. If, however, the losses ( − ) outweigh the gains ( + ), then perhaps it is time to retreat, reconsider, and reinvent. Good innovators do not look for "sure things," but they like to have the odds in their favor. They want to know that the + 's are greater than the − 's. This is the last checkpoint in the Change Checklist – step 20. See Figure 5.21 for an illustration of risk analysis. If the + 's of Form 13 outweigh the − 's, go ahead and begin your action plan. The time has come to stop planning and start doing.

| RISK ANALYSIS | CLP PROJECT |
|---|---|
| **Gains from Change Effort** | **How many + 's?**<br>( +, + +, + + +, or + + + + ) |
| 1. Better manager direction of workers | + + |
| 2. Better manager relations with board | + + + |
| 3. Better manager relations with outside clients | + + + |
| 4. Better worker understanding of orders and directions | + + + + |
| 5. Promotability of staff | + + |
| 6. Team sense | + |
| **Losses from Change Effort** | **How many − 's?**<br>( −, − −, − − −, or − − − − ) |
| 1. Time | − − |
| 2. Turnover of those who resist literacy | − |
| 3. Money | − − |
| Do + 's outweigh − 's? Yes, 15 to 5. | |

*Figure 5.21. Sample risk analysis (Form 13).*

## SUMMARY

Too often a change strategy is pictured as something to do. It is not. It is a series of things to analyze, plan, and then implement. The change process is made up of a series of steps that add up to change. The Change Checklist in Figure 5.22 summarizes those steps that will give you the greatest probability for success. Following the checklist is a series of supporting forms that lead you through the twenty steps in the checklist. There is nothing magical about the process, the steps, the checklist, or the forms. They are presented merely as a systematic means of increasing the probability of successful change.

In fact, in Appendix B, you will find a shortened checklist. In most cases, the fuller version is recommended, but you may have occasion to take the shorter. There is nothing magical about either, as long as you remember and apply the fundamental principles of change.

| Analysis | Subsidiary Form |
|---|---|
| ☐ 1. Description:<br>What is the change?<br>Is it clear and understandable? | Form 1 |
| ☐ 2. Need:<br>Is there a need for change? | Form 1 |
| ☐ 3. Potential actors:<br>Who are the changers?<br>Who are the changees? | Form 2 |
| ☐ 4. Payoff<br>What's in it for the changee? | Form 3 |
| ☐ 5. Unfreezing.<br>☐ Strain<br>☐ Potency<br>☐ Valence | Form 4 |
| ☐ 6. Resistance.<br>What are the sources of resistance? | Form 5 |
| ☐ 7. Investment.<br>Who already supports change? | Form 6 |
| ☐ 8. Culture:<br>Does the organizational culture support change? | Form 6 |

**Planning**

| | |
|---|---|
| ☐ 9. Actual changees:<br>What actors are actually going to be changed? | Form 7 |
| ☐ 10. Change strategy:<br>☐ Rational–empirical<br>☐ Power–coercive<br>☐ Normative–reeducative | Form 8 |

*Figure 5.22. Change checklist.*

| Analysis | Subsidiary Form |
|---|---|
| ☐ 11. Resistance strategy: | Form 8 |
| How is resistance to be dealt with? | |
| ☐ 12. Participation: | Form 9 |
| How is involvement to be generated? | |
| ☐ 13. Excitement: | Form 9 |
| How is excitement to be generated? | |
| ☐ 14. Change environment: | Form 9 |
| How does change fit broader patterns of change? | |
| ☐ 15. Scope: | Form 10 |
| Is the effort too trivial or too big? | |

**Implementation and Evaluation**

| | |
|---|---|
| ☐ 16. Advocates: | Form 11 |
| Who are the visible advocates for the change? | |
| ☐ 17. Time frame: | Form 11 |
| What is the time frame for planning and implementation? | |
| ☐ 18. Monitoring: | Form 11 |
| How will the change be monitored? Who is responsible for monitoring? | |
| ☐ 19. Action plan: | Form 12 |
| What are the precise who's, what's, and when's of the change process? | |
| ☐ 20. Risk analysis: | Form 13 |
| Do gains (+) outweigh losses (−)? | |

*Figure 5.22 (continued). Change checklist.*

## Change Checklist
## Form 1.
## Change and Need

Describe the intended change in one paragraph:

What facts show the need for this change?

1.

2.

3.

4.

5.

6.

7.

## Change Checklist
## Form 2.
## Potential Changees

| Name | Position | Reason for Listing as Potential Changee |
|---|---|---|
| 1. | | |
| 2. | | |
| 3. | | |
| 4. | | |
| 5. | | |
| 6. | | |
| 7. | | |
| 8. | | |
| 9. | | |
| 10. | | |
| 11. | | |
| 12. | | |
| 13. | | |
| 14. | | |
| 15. | | |
| 16. | | |
| 17. | | |
| 18. | | |
| 19. | | |
| 20. | | |

**Change Checklist**
**Form 3.**
**Payoff Analysis**

| Name of Changee | Potential Payoffs |
|---|---|
| 1. _____ | _____ |
| 2. _____ | _____ |
| 3. _____ | _____ |
| 4. _____ | _____ |
| 5. _____ | _____ |
| 6. _____ | _____ |
| 7. _____ | _____ |
| 8. _____ | _____ |
| 9. _____ | _____ |
| 10. _____ | _____ |

## Change Checklist
## Form 4.
## Readiness for Unfreezing

| Name of Changee | Appropriate Strain? (Yes/No) | Positive Valence? (Yes/No) | Adequate Potency? (Yes/No) |
|---|---|---|---|
| 1. | | | |
| 2. | | | |
| 3. | | | |
| 4. | | | |
| 5. | | | |
| 6. | | | |
| 7. | | | |
| 8. | | | |

STRAIN:

VALENCE:

POTENCY:

## Change Checklist
## Form 5.
## Potential Resistance Factors

| In this change effort, to what extent do you find: | - Driving → Change ← Restraining - | | | | |
| --- | --- | --- | --- | --- | --- |
| | Not at all | | | | Very much so |
| Lack of ownership | 1 | 2 | 3 | 4 | 5 |
| Lack of benefits | 1 | 2 | 3 | 4 | 5 |
| Increased burdens | 1 | 2 | 3 | 4 | 5 |
| Lack of top brass support | 1 | 2 | 3 | 4 | 5 |
| Loneliness | 1 | 2 | 3 | 4 | 5 |
| Insecurity | 1 | 2 | 3 | 4 | 5 |
| Norm incongruence | 1 | 2 | 3 | 4 | 5 |
| Boredom | 1 | 2 | 3 | 4 | 5 |
| Chaos | 1 | 2 | 3 | 4 | 5 |
| Superiority | 1 | 2 | 3 | 4 | 5 |
| Differential knowledge | 1 | 2 | 3 | 4 | 5 |
| Lack of recognition | 1 | 2 | 3 | 4 | 5 |
| Sudden, wholesale change | 1 | 2 | 3 | 4 | 5 |
| Failure | 1 | 2 | 3 | 4 | 5 |
| Extremes of organizational structure | 1 | 2 | 3 | 4 | 5 |
| Unique sources | 1 | 2 | 3 | 4 | 5 |

Any factors rated 4 or 5 are resistance factors needing attention.

## Change Checklist
## Form 6.
## Supporters and Culture

**LIST OF SUPPORTERS**

**Name**                                              **Reason for Listing as Supporter**

1. _____

2. _____

3. _____

4. _____

5. _____

6. _____

7. _____

8. _____

**Description of Culture for Change**

## Change Checklist
## Form 7.
## Actual Changees

Rate each changee using the scales indicated. The three factors are:

- Degree of influence/input in the organization
- Need to be changed
- Degree of changeability

| Name of Potential Changee | Influence Low → High 1 – 9 | Need Low → High 1 – 9 | Changeability Low → High 1 – 5 | Total |
|---|---|---|---|---|
| 1. | | | | |
| 2. | | | | |
| 3. | | | | |
| 4. | | | | |
| 5. | | | | |
| 6. | | | | |
| 7. | | | | |
| 8. | | | | |
| 9. | | | | |
| 10. | | | | |
| 11. | | | | |
| 12. | | | | |
| 13. | | | | |
| 14. | | | | |

As a guideline, select as actual changees those candidates with a total score of 13 or more.

## Change Checklist
## Form 8.
## Strategy Sheet

---

**CHANGE STRATEGY**

- RE = rational–empirical
- PC = power–coercive
- NR = normative–reeducative

**RESISTANCE STRATEGY**

**High-Scoring Sources of
Resistance (see Form 5)**                                   **Response**

---

## Change Checklist
## Form 9.
## Participation, Excitement, and Change Environment

How do you plan to create:

Participation?

Excitement?

Where does this effort fit into the pattern of change?

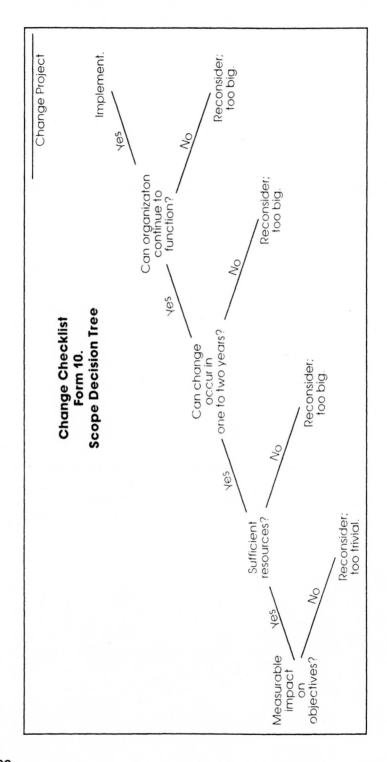

**Change Checklist
Form 10.
Scope Decision Tree**

Change Project

Measurable
impact
on
objectives?

Yes → Sufficient resources?

No → Reconsider; too trivial.

Sufficient resources?

Yes → Can change occur in one to two years?

No → Reconsider; too big.

Can change occur in one to two years?

Yes → Can organizaton continue to function?

No → Reconsider; too big.

Can organizaton continue to function?

Yes → Implement.

No → Reconsider; too big.

## Change Checklist
## Form 11.
## Responsibility Chart

Advocates for change    1. _____

                              2. _____

                              3. _____

Time frame               _____

When to begin?         _____

When to complete?      _____

Dates of interim
    reports (if needed)     _____

How will the change be monitored?    By whom?

## Change Checklist
## Form 12.
## Action Plan

| Number | Action Step | Who Is Involved? | Resources Needed? | When? |
|--------|-------------|------------------|-------------------|-------|
| 1. | | | | |
| 2. | | | | |
| 3. | | | | |
| 4. | | | | |
| 5. | | | | |
| 6. | | | | |
| 7. | | | | |
| 8. | | | | |

**Change Checklist**
**Form 13.**
**Risk Analysis**

**Gains from Change Effort**

**How many + 's?**
**( +, + +, + + +, or + + + + )**

1.

2.

3.

4.

5.

6.

7.

**Losses from Change Effort**

**How many − 's?**
**( −, − −, − − −, or − − − − )**

1.

2.

3.

4.

5.

6.

Do + 's outweigh − 's?

The + 's and − 's are meant as a simple approximation of the degree of gain and loss from the change effort. They are not exact measurements but are approximations of importance (like four-star restaurants or five-star hotels or a Likert scale).

# CHAPTER 6

# Institutionalization of Change

CREATING change is not enough. You must also worry about how to keep the change in place—how to insure its survival beyond the initial enthusiasm or after the seed money disappears. In other words, you are now faced with institutionalization of change—integration of a change effort into the mainstream of the organization so that its continuance is at least as certain as that of any other activity in the organization.

We have all seen myriad reforms and innovations that arrived on the scene with much tumultuous fanfare but have just as quickly evaporated into the mists of history. The reality is documented in the "Whatever Happened To. . ." series that appeared in *Phi Delta Kappan* in 1981-1982. The world of reform, in fact, is like that legendary Brigadoon—a wondrous place that rises from the mist once every 100 years and disappears at the end of the day, not to be seen for yet another century. Many changes come and go. Few last.

In the last chapter, an approach to change that takes much thought and time was proposed. If you are going to do all that work, and if you believe in the value of the change you seek, then should it not last? Change worth doing is worth institutionalizing. In this chapter, I suggest factors that lead to institutionalization and, therefore, increase the probability of lasting change.

## FUNDAMENTAL PREMISE

You cannot institutionalize a change after you have implemented it. You must do so before you implement. I have addressed this fundamental premise in previous research projects (Lucas and Harvey, 1984; Curtis, Harvey, and Kuhns, 1978). Each such revisitation convinces me of its truth. The probability that a change will survive depends upon analyzing and planning for change in advance, not on strategizing after the fact. If you do not set the stage for institutionalization while you are planning and implementing, chances are low that it will occur later.

In reviewing and researching 250 change efforts—some funded externally, some internally—eight fundamental determinants of institutionalizing change have been found. Each of these will be described. Build them into your change effort and watch the new idea take root and grow strong!

## PLANNING AND PREPARATION

Many managers have the John Wayne or Clint Eastwood vision of change—"Move it out, now . . . roll 'em up . . . rawhide . . . get it goin'." They are impatient with inefficient, slow-moving folks. They see themselves as movers and shakers. They want to make something happen. Any one of us might fall prey to this seductive image. It is exhilarating. But it works against long-term survival. Careful project planning is time-consuming, frustrating, and far from efficient. If you want change to last, to become institutionalized, then invest the necessary self-discipline, time, and effort.

Now what are the elements of careful planning and preparation? There is nothing magical about them. They are:

(1) Listening—Willingness to seek out others and actively hear what they have to say

(2) Involving—Participation of many people in defining the what and how of change

(3) Directing—Organization of the disparate work of individuals; ability to meld and give focus to a task team

(4) Analyzing—Capacity to receive, sort, and aggregate information and ideas to make sense

(5) Crafting—Artisanship in shaping information and values into a product that satisfies identified needs and interests

These five elements may be performed at different times in various settings. There is often the classic accordion process (see Figure 6.1).

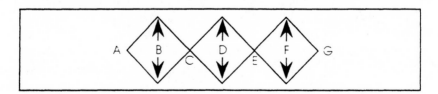

*Figure 6.1.* The accordion process.

Like the closing and opening of the bellows on an accordion, a small group/team first defines a tentative change vision (point A), then widens out to get input on that vision from a broad array of potential changees (point B). The results are returned to the small group (point C) for analysis, focus, and crafting. This cycle will typically be replicated (points C through G) until sufficient listening and involvement have occurred. This back-and-forth process insures increased investment in and understanding of the change vision.

But all this discussion is time-consuming. Clearly, to define and impose the change by oneself, autocratically, would be more efficient. But in this circumstance changees will not understand it, will not accept it, and will probably sabotage it. In looking at changes that last, I have found that careful planning and participation are strong indicants of successful institutionalization.

## TIMING

Every great athlete, every great musician, knows that timing is everything. All the skills in the world cannot overcome being at the wrong place at the wrong time. The same is true of great change agents. Funding and approval processes often contribute to poor timing. Two college situations come to mind as examples of ineffective timing.

(1) A small midwestern college wanted to institute a social consciousness program in 1969. By the time they were approved for funding, it was 1973. They opened the program, but only two students enrolled. The students of 1969 were vastly different from those of 1973. Interest had shifted in this brief four-year period from social intervention to personal economic needs. The college simply missed the targeted opportunity because of timing.

(2) I evaluated an excellent eastern college with an interesting $300,000 general education project. The project, however, was a dismal failure. The problem was that in the preceding year the college had merged with another school and the merger was not going smoothly. There were too many organizational adjustments to allow the general education project to succeed. Timing was terrible.

In any organization—whether college, hospital, business, or governmental agency—changes that last occur at the right moment in the history of the organization. However skilled your advance planning, if the propitious moment has passed, you may need to hold off or even abandon the change effort. When timing is right, then proceed.

## CONGRUENCE WITH MISSION

Too many changes start at the margin or periphery of the organization—and end where they began. Changes that last are congruent with the central mission of the institution. Note the word *central*. No institution is ever fully static in its purpose, function, or mission because it must respond to new demands and interests dictated by today's turbulent environment. But, if *all* needs and functions shift, then the institution is simply irresolute, driven by current fads. To maintain equilibrium in a turbulent environment, an organization must know the sine qua non—that which stays consistent—in its mission. The more the change relates or links to that central, unchanging core of the mission, the more likely its survival in the face of shifting, but less central, priorities.

Funded projects are particularly sensitive to these shifting priorities. When money is available, one thinks, Why not create a new program to capture some of those dollars? But if, when the *soft* money runs out, the program does not match the main budgetary and programmatic thrusts of the organization, its chance for survival is limited. When soft money creates an *itch*, and one responds, problems of institutionalization are great. It is much better if the itch is there before the funds become available to scratch it!

Changes that last, funded or not, are those which address genuine need. Someone must be skeptical enough to ask, "Is this really central to the mission of our organization?" If the answer is yes, then it can survive the vagaries of reprioritization, RIF, new reforms, and national studies.

## ENVIRONMENTAL SENSITIVITY

Environmental sensitivity is the flip side of congruence with mission. First, a crash course in systems theory.

Systems theory defines open and closed systems (Kast and Rosenzweig, 1985). Closed systems receive their inputs and needs assessments from constituencies and mechanisms contained within the organization. They are internally focused. Open systems, on the other hand, receive direction partly from within but largely from without the organization. They are externally focused.

In static environments closed systems work well (Burns and Stalker, 1961). But in turbulent environments—in environments characterized by numerous conflicting or ambiguous demands, changes, and politics—closed systems tend to be increasingly entropic. Eventually, they die. Open systems survive better in turbulent environments.

Thus, systems theory explains the principle of environmental sensitivity, which is in turn a reality of institutionalizing change. Changes that last are largely responsive to external demands and needs. Because we live in a volatile, demanding world, our organizational changes must reflect the changing world around us. When universities look only to faculty in defining change, or hospitals to doctors, or government agencies to the bureaucrats, then they are doomed either to no change at all, or to closed-system changes with little hope of success or survival.

Nevertheless, although organizations must be environmentally sensitive, they cannot be environmentally dependent. If everything they do is a function of external demands, then they will succumb to every fad and fancy in the turbulent outside world. Changes that last walk the middle road—they are sensitive to, but not dependent on, the environment.

## CLARITY AND SIMPLICITY

As noted in the preceding chapter, one of the real problems with change is language. Most changers do not want to use simple English. They would rather write in jargon and obtuse language. A dilemma in writing this book was that the more conversational I made it (the more I spoke to you in plain English), the less likely a publisher would be to accept it for publication. But if I do not write in English, you, the reader, will not stick with me long enough to find out about my ideas. I have opted for plain English. If you are reading this, my strategy must have worked.

Why not impress changees with polysyllabic abstractions and architectonic amphibologies? Because, as the question itself shows, they confuse and distract people. The more ambiguous or obtuse the description of change, the more likely everyone will express agreement, for the message is read by individuals as each person prefers. Language that obscures intent, rather than clarifying, may work for early acceptance of the change, but eventually conflicting interpretations emerge and the happy coalition falls apart.

State reforms are glorious examples of obscurity. Whole consulting industries have been formed on the need to interpret governmental demands and reforms. If a legislature or congress does not use broad, vague language, then they will not generate sufficient votes for passage. But doesn't that tell you something? It tells you that political agreements usually represent fake, not real consensus. For lasting change, needs, intentions, and payoffs must be stated clearly and simply. They must be readily understood by everyone. This clarity may surface disagreements, but that is an advantage. Open disagreement enables you to identify the resisters and analyze the sources of their resistance. If you want lasting change, it is important to articulate that change in clear, simple language—to fight the fight of consensus early, before the implementation stage.

## UNPRETENTIOUS REALISM

"This reform will change the face of education". . . or health care or business or whatever. We have all become weary and skeptical of overblown, pretentious change efforts. Change agents who feel they must sell the change effort as incredibly significant or historic or earth-shattering forget that most of us know that any single change yields limited impact. Therefore, the more realistically we speak of change, the more believable we are.

A further caution—even if we succeed at inspiring faith in an overblown, pretentious change effort, eventually we will disappoint our supporters. We may deliver modifications, even important modifications, but seldom can we generate transformations. Realism works.

Look at marriages that last. Not many brides see the groom as a cross between Adonis and Albert Einstein (with a touch of Don Juan, perhaps). Nor do most grooms see the bride as a blend of Venus, Madame Curie, and Julia Childs. More important, if you somehow convince your spouse that you are such a paragon, you know you likely cannot deliver on that image and your spouse will soon be disappointed. Research on successful, long-term marriages suggests the importance of accepting imperfection. Realism works!

In proposing a change effort, acknowledge imperfections and limitations. This is not to suggest that the objective is unimportant or unworthy—just that it is not perfect. It will solve some problems, but not all. Your change effort is not Prince Charming, but then neither is it a toad. It is simply good and useful and, I hope, fun.

## SUFFICIENT, NOT INDULGENT RESOURCES

Most of us recognize that many change efforts are undercapitalized. Some, however, are overcapitalized—a situation equally problematic.

In reviewing 104 funded change efforts for the National Endowment for the Humanities (Curtis, Harvey, and Kuhns, 1978), we found an interesting phenomenon with respect to evaluation. We expected to find more money for evaluation associated with better evaluations. We did not find this to be true, particularly when we used the criterion that a good evaluation is useful for making decisions and redirecting programs. (Remember that evaluation differs from research in its usability characteristic. Evaluation that is not used is not effective. It may be good research, but it is not good evaluation.) Figure 6.2 shows the relationship between money and impact of the evaluation.

In my research, I found the greatest impact *not* where the money was greatest, but where it was quite modest (Curtis, Harvey, and Kuhns, 1978). Why? When you have a generous budget for evaluation, where does it go? The money is frequently expended on outside consultants

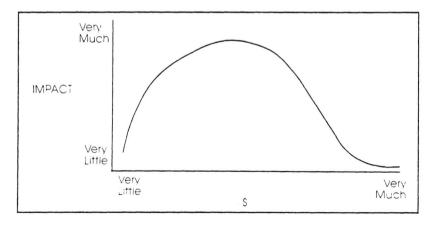

*Figure 6.2.* Relationship between cost of an evaluation and its impact on program direction.

and complex designs, resulting in decreased involvement of internal personnel and increased complexity and obtuseness of results. When money was quite modest, internal workers had to do more of the work with less complex designs. The result of a small (but not minuscule) evaluation budget was greater understanding, higher investment in the findings, and stronger commitment to pursuing their implications.

Our study is consistent with Barker's intriguing and often overlooked set of findings (1968). Barker classified personnel allocations as overmanned, optimally manned, or undermanned, with "optimally manned" described as having the right number of people for necessary functions. The expected finding is that optimally manned is best and undermanned the worst. This expectation was consistently refuted. Achievement, responsibility, productivity, satisfaction, and the like were highest when organizations were moderately undermanned! In essence, the more we are needed, the better we produce. The worst condition was the overmanned one. No one took responsibility because he/she was sure that someone else would do so.

The implication of these findings for institutionalization of change is that modest resources support long-term change. No business that is undercapitalized can survive even for days. No change can survive without modest allocations of budget, time, and energy.

But those allocations need not be immense. Modest resources force invention, investment, and organizational commitment. Vast resources may well create long-term problems:

- Spending too much of the organization's scarce resources on one effort shortchanges the rest of the organization.
- Money as a payoff tends to be short-term; if you are buying commitment, the change will probably not last.
- Vast expenditures of time and energy make for great sprints but poor marathons; marathon runners last until institutionalization, but sprinters do not.

Therefore, change agents need to generate sufficient, but not indulgent, resources. Realistic, modest allocations of money, time, and energy lead to lasting change.

## STRONG, CENTRAL LEADERSHIP

As I discussed in Chapter 5, advocacy is a critical issue in creating change. Beyond that, a particular attitude in advocacy is most productive for institutionalizing change.

Take a university, for instance. In that setting three types of leaders spell disaster for long-term change – the untenured faculty member trying to start a program as a toehold in the organization, the empire-builder looking for self-aggrandizement, and the person resisting redirection onto a siding as a solution to a leadership problem elsewhere. Every organization has its own versions of these change agents who see change as a personal steppingstone. But although change may advance an individual's career, it should not be sought for that purpose – at least not if you care about institutionalizing the change.

The ideal project leader is not a marginal member on the make or an individual whose ego is more important than the outcome. Rather, effective change agents are individuals already trusted and respected in the organization, persons who are linked into the central mission and goals of the organization. Such a leader must serve as a lightning rod for ideas and activities and articulate the reasons for change throughout the lifespan of the project. Change efforts with such a leader achieve long-term survival. Without that leadership, program survival is compromised.

## REDUCED INDIVIDUAL PROPRIETARY INTEREST

This final element of institutionalization is inversely related to the previous one – strong, central leadership. While an effective advocate is necessary for change, that person's proprietary interest must be kept at the lowest level, consistent with his or her personal commitment and satisfaction. Shares in the project must be "sold." Ownership must move from the few to the many. In that way, when an individual moves, shifts attention, grows tired, loses face, gets fired or promoted, or whatever, the program does not die. Links established throughout the organization form a web of support.

I recall a change effort in an art institute. My first step on being named consultant was to form an internal team and tell them that I could not analyze the circumstances or create the change. I could only help them to do it. Nearly everyone strongly resented the notion of change and was openly suspicious of the team. In fact, it was commonly referred to as the Harvey Task Force – and that was not meant to be a compliment! We did our work, much as described in Chapter 5, and we began to have small successes. By the time we completed the entire process, the newspaper had carried several articles describing our success. These articles referred to "the Faculty

| Change Steps | Planning and Preparation | Timing | Congruence with Mission | Environmental Sensitivity | Clear and Simple | Realism | Sufficient Resources | Central Leader | Reduced Proprietary Interest |
|---|---|---|---|---|---|---|---|---|---|
| Description | X | | X | X | X | X | | | |
| Need | X | X | X | X | X | X | | | |
| Potential actors | X | | | | | | | X | X |
| Payoff | X | | | | | X | X | | |
| Unfreezing | X | | | | | X | | | |
| Resistance | X | | | | | X | | | |
| Investment | X | | | X | | | X | | X |
| Culture | X | | | X | | | | | X |
| Actual changees | X | | | | | | | | |
| Change strategy | X | | | | X | | X | | |
| Resistance strategy | X | | | | X | | X | | X |
| Participation | X | | | X | | | X | | |
| Excitement | X | | | | | | | | |
| Pattern of change | X | | | | | X | | | X |
| Scope | X | X | | | | X | X | | |
| Advocate | X | | | | | | | X | |
| Time frame | X | X | | | | X | X | | |
| Monitoring | X | | | | | | | | |
| Action plans | X | | | | | | X | | X |
| Risk | X | | | | | | X | | X |

Figure 6.3. *Relationship between change steps and institutionalization factors.*

Task Force, aided by a consultant." They no longer even mentioned my name! The greedy part of me yearned for more tributes, but the knowledgeable part of me understood that I had succeeded in moving the change from myself to a wider group.

A change agent needs a strong ego. If you expect unremitting tributes, then you probably will fail to spread responsibility and ownership for the change and, thus, will fall short of long-term change. You need to reduce individual property interest and extend ownership to the many.

## CONCLUDING NOTE

The nine elements of institutionalization tie into the steps of the Change Checklist in Chapter 5. The matrix in Figure 6.3 on the following page relates the two sets of variables. The most influential determinant of institutionalization, and hence, of long-term change, is the first one, planning and preparation. But all are important. All deserve attention as you proceed through the Change Checklist. If a change is so important that you are willing to devote your attention and energies to its accomplishments, then it is important enough to keep around for a long time.

# CHAPTER 7

# How to Keep from Being a Victim
# of Change

CHANGE is a fascinating subject to most of us, partly because we are interested in creating it, but also because we are so often its victim. Most of us are bombarded by change efforts every week, every month, every year. We are frustrated by the array of demands cast upon us, and we long for more control. We feel violated, confused, and deeply resistant.

This chapter is dedicated to all those frustrated managers and subordinates who feel battered and overwhelmed by change but somehow feel it is not legitimate to openly resist "progress." Change sometimes equals progress; sometimes it does not.

In reality, we are, at times, victims of change.

- Sometimes it's the speed of change that creates confusion. The faster a car goes, the less reaction time one has and the more terrifying the effects of faulty judgment. Faced with repeated fast-paced change, we feel like a car out of control and struggle to bring caution to a headstrong world.
- Sometimes it's a case of having our expectations violated. We plan on things working out in certain ways with certain benefits and certain people. Then everything changes. This is a disconcerting attack on hope and expectations. It is only those without experience or hope who have no expectations. They are the only ones for whom change is no problem. For the rest of us, we need our hopes and a tempered belief that things will turn out as planned.
- Sometimes it's the loss of control that terrifies us. We work in organizations because we believe in organized activities; we believe in coordination and cooperation. Change that attacks our sense of control also attacks our faith in our organizations and our ability to collaborate. Think of terms like "out of control," "uncontrolling," or "uncontrollable." When these are applied to

people or programs, they terrify us. Belief in the capacity for reasonable control is the basis for self-governance and mutual support. Anything that attacks that belief makes us feel like victims.

- Sometimes it's the increased burdens that frustrate us. Almost all change I have experienced entails more time, effort, and money—three scarce resources. The more you take from me, the more frustrated and resistant I become.
- Change always says "Something new is better. What you believed to be better is no longer true." Whenever you attack people's belief, you attack them personally. Research is clear that value conflict is the most difficult to resolve and the most affronting.
- Sometimes change is simply an assault on security, real or imagined. What I have been doing for ten years in the same way may be boring, but it is incredibly secure. When change comes, it brings more excitement and possibilities for growth, but it also brings insecurity. Will I be able to learn the new way? Will I be needed? Will I be included?

For all these reasons, and probably many more, people feel like victims of change. And victims fight back sooner or later. This chapter suggests that we need to avoid being a victim, that we need to find ways to deal with all the changes thrust on us.

There are eight points I want to make about this issue.

(1) It is okay to resist change.

(2) Strategies for controlling change are mirror images of strategies for creating change.

(3) Exploiting someone else's change is sane and desirable.

(4) If you don't want to be run over by the parade, be in front of it.

(5) Define problem ownership.

(6) Call time out daily.

(7) Have fun.

(8) Congruency analysis is a key to eliminating the need for change.

## O.K. TO RESIST

Perhaps I have belabored the point; nonetheless, let me say it again—resistance to change is not inappropriate. To avoid being a victim of change, know that your initial resistance is quite sane. You need not feel guilty nor angry about a change you do not like. Without payoff to you or your institution, you have the right and responsibility to say no. The fact that the changer—be it the CEO, legislature, a board, or the boss—is unable to articulate a strategy that provides incentive for you does not mean you are at fault. Consider another wonderful old adage, "Poor planning on your part does not necessitate an emergency on my part."

Someone else's inability to effect meaningful change should not create a problem for you. You simply need to resist—coolly and rationally. If you become angry, frustrated, or insecure, then the problem becomes yours. But many an excellent, sane, sensible manager or superordinate simply outwaits an ineffective change agent.

## REVERSE CHANGE STRATEGIES

Strategies to block change are simply mirror images of those described in Chapters 4 and 5. Instead of moving from point A to a potential point B, you want to move from a potential point B to point A. To do this you need to:

(1) Describe what you want. Establish the need to stay where you are. What is positive about point A?

(2) Know the actors in the process and provide payoff to them to maintain the status quo.

(3) Resolve conflict effectively and reduce strain in the organization. Without strain, unfreezing the organization is difficult.

(4) Understand why you and others resist and make sure your reasons are legitimate and productive to the organization.

(5) Support involvement in maintaining the structure and achieving the goals of the organization.

(6) Maintain an enjoyable climate that fulfills individual and group needs.

These are but a few of the available strategies to block change. All mirror the facilitating strategies outlined in earlier chapters and hinge on an effective, functional organization. Avoiding change will be tough if your organization is unproductive, dispirited, and hostile. In that case, you need to be a victim of change. But if you manage a healthy organization faced with countering an unnecessary or redundant change effort, simply turn the Change Checklist around.

## EXPLOIT THE POSSIBILITIES

If a change effort is clearly defined and its implementation precisely laid out, then there is little room for manager discretion and judgment. Few imposed changes fall into this category. In fact, imposed changes are so exasperating precisely because they are obtuse and poorly planned and coordinated.

But this very ambiguity is fertile ground for you. Exploit the opportunities so handily provided! For example, if the state legislature mandates public advisory committees, a principal might ask, "How can I use this opportunity to achieve what *I* want?" Exploit the occasion by linking the mandate with your personal vision of the organization. Again, if a hospital board mandates quality circle programs, the manager can use these same circles to accomplish his or her purposes. I do not suggest that you pervert the basic thrust of the mandated change but, rather, that you fulfill your personal organizational agenda while also implementing the mandate from above. In that way, rather than a victim of someone else's change, you become the co-agent in useful organizational change.

## LEAD THE PARADE

There is another wonderful old adage (I hope you have noticed how much I like old adages) that goes, "If you don't want to be run over by the parade, be in front of it." When you anticipate events, you are more likely to control them. People least likely to be victims of change are those who consistently scan the environment for new ideas, realities, or trends. They see what is coming and prepare themselves. For the time when you do not see something coming is the time you will be hurt the most. Think of a tackle in football or a broken marriage or loss of a job or a shift in political power or an irresponsible driver. We cannot always avoid the negative impact, but we can lessen it by anticipating. And indeed, in some cases we can even avoid the disaster entirely.

We live in a world of open systems surrounded by a turbulent environment. Therefore, change often comes from outside our organization. Hospitals have adapted the notions of marketing and market segments in an effort to deal with their environments. Strategic planning and environmental scanning are clear priorities in industry. These entities recognize that anticipating the environment is the only way to avert disaster and control their organization. In education, too, nearly all fundamental reforms have come from outside. Educators, therefore, must anticipate changes and lead the parade to avoid becoming victims of change.

## DEFINE PROBLEM OWNERSHIP

Have you ever fallen prey to the following situation? The children in the neighborhood start fighting. The parents are drawn into the dispute and take on the fight. While the parents' hostility grows, the two kids go off to play. We have all seen this hundreds of times—one person taking over the problem of another, only to see things worsen.

The same is true of change. You see a change in the life of a friend, relative, co-worker, community member or whomever, and you become incensed for them. You read something in the newspaper and mutter, "What's the world coming to?" You encounter an issue about which you have very little information, but immediately you jump to a solution. Many changes that frustrate us are simply none of our business. Being neither divine nor all-absorbing, we should tend to our own changes, not those of others. A certain personal arrogance is involved in presuming that I should be involved in others' problems and others' changes—that they are not capable of coping with their own worlds. This is not to say we should ignore the plight of others, but that we should more carefully pick our fights, more carefully choose the changes to resist! Otherwise, we dissipate our energy and our power to affect anything. When you try to intrude into too many changes and problems, you become a victim. And victims cannot be effective.

## CALL A TIMEOUT DAILY

No matter what anybody else may say, recess was always the best part of school; vacation is a lot more fun than work; parties are more delightful than meetings; and the worst day at golf is better than the best day at work. Somehow we forget this. One of the most important things executives can do is to call a timeout daily. Each of us needs at least thirty to sixty minutes each working day to do nothing "productive." We might play gin, putt, go for a walk, nap, shoot baskets, paint, play the piano, or whatever—we need to stop and refuel psychically. When you feel yourself being overwhelmed by change, don't count to ten, count to a thousand, or better yet, do something dumb. The most productive thing you can do is to be *un*productive.

## HAVE FUN

Chapter 2 said, "If you want change, have a party." That sentence could be changed to "If you want to avoid being a victim of change, have a party." Now, don't misunderstand; this does not mean that life is one big party. But the more joy you bring into each activity, the more productive and the less victimized you'll be. Let me recite a trivial example—the Little League snack bar.

In my son's Little League, each team must take its turn at working in the snack bar. This is the parental version of being sent to Devil's Island. In our town, as in many others, the snack bar has a permanent supervisor whom we affectionately call "she who must be obeyed" (SWMBO), à la Horace Rumpole. Well, every time something breaks or goes wrong, SWMBO flies into a fit and creates hell for all the volunteers. I have always felt that it was my job to turn that snack bar duty into a whopping good time. So I kidded and cajoled my fellow volunteers and bugged SWMBO every time she flew into a rage. I cooked hamburgers with verve and teased the kids coming to the window for the fourteenth piece of licorice. The result was always the same—volunteers were more productive, time went faster, SWMBO was less irritating, and the whole organization ran better.

You are less often a victim when you seize control of the environment and make it a vital, exciting place. An atmosphere of boredom, dismay, and hostility breeds victims!

## ANALYZE FOR CONGRUENCY

There are hosts of ways to assess needs. Probably the most common method is discrepancy analysis—a comparison of the actual state with the ideal state to determine significant discrepancies. These discrepancies then become the *needs* – the agenda for change. An obvious outcome of this approach is, the more discrepancies, the more change efforts – until the organization is bombarded by change. Conversely, of course, the fewer the discrepancies, the less the push for change.

If you do not wish to be overwhelmed by change, then manage your organization for maximum congruence between the actual and ideal states. Congruency management means a healthier organization and a healthier manager. Managers who complain that they are victims of change have not looked for discrepancies in their organization. They assume that silence means congruency, satisfaction with the status quo. That is rarely true. Rather than being lulled into complacency because no one is complaining, ask questions. Rather than assume congruency, manage it!

## CONCLUDING NOTE

At this point, some may ask, "Why in a book on change are you counseling people on how to block or avoid change?" That is a good question, with equally good answers. First, not all changes are desirable. Stalin was a change agent, but certainly not benign. Other changes I have found worth resisting or blocking are punk rock, purple hair, zero-based budgeting, state centralization of school funding, the Pinto, loans to Brazil, airline deregulation, and on and on and on. You may not agree with my list – you undoubtedly have your own – but perhaps we agree that some things, whatever they may be, are not worth accepting.

Second, too much change causes an unhealthy situation. Burnout, stress, and breakdowns occur in the face of excessive change. Layne Longfellow cites research showing that 70 percent of all convicted felons went through significant social change in their lives in the twelve months prior to their crime. This figure was significantly higher than that in the noncriminal population. Just for sanity's sake, sometimes you need to resist change.

Third, most of this chapter talks about the need to manage operations more effectively. Many changes are due to outside agencies meddling in our organizations because we have failed to maintain them effectively. We are bombarded with changes because of our own shortcomings. Better managed organizations need less change.

Finally, this chapter has consistently emphasized the issue of control.

Each of us yearns strongly for control for ourselves and our institutions. We feel most victimized and hence, inept, when we feel loss of control. By exercising control, you can accept and use change better. Remember, change is not a goal in and of itself, but only to the degree that it advances the goals of the organization and fulfills the needs of individuals and groups within the organization. Therefore, sometimes you want to create change and sometimes you want to control it. Would you teach your youngster to use only the gas pedal on your car? Of course not—without brakes, he is not a complete driver. An effective change agent needs both to create and to control change.

# PART III

# MANAGING CHANGE TEAMS

# CHAPTER 8

# Using Teams for Change

EARLIER in this book I noted that the most effective change endeavors are team efforts. The reasons for this have probably become obvious. For one thing, decision theory tells us that multiple inputs and multiple decision makers improve the quality of the decision (Harrison, 1981; Tosi, 1986). No one person can know it all. In addition, a team approach broadens the range of investment in the outcome, and investment is critical to change. Additionally, a team approach expands available resources—time and energy—and, hence, the potential scope of the change effort.

For these reasons I argue that every change effort should be pursued through a collaborative team process and that this sense of collaboration should expand beyond team members to all those significantly affected by the decision. In some cases these teams may be already established groups or standing committees, but in my experience, existing groups rarely function as the most effective strategists for change. Most change teams are ad hoc bodies that are formed for a particular reason and exist solely for that change effort.

Note, however, that it is sometimes difficult to let ad hoc groups die their natural death. Colleagues who have worked well and hard together resist giving up those associations and successes, but they must. Once the change is implemented and institutionalized, it is time for the team to move on. The rest of this chapter will deal with forming and using an ad hoc change team.

## FORMING THE TEAM

A frequent dilemma in team formation is the Noah's Ark syndrome—having two of every constituency represented on the team. This larger group probably results in the outcome Noah faced: At the end of it all we are left high and dry on a mountain top. Team formation requires more focused planning.

## Size

Change teams should consist of five to twelve members (Peters and Waterman, 1982). You need at least five for a variety of ideas and disagreements. You also need five in case of attrition or self-destruction. Conversely, you should limit your group to twelve members. Research on group dynamics demonstrates that groups larger than that tend to split into subgroups and become unmanageable. Cohesion and communication are very important in this process; teams of five to twelve are optimal for these processes.

## Composition

The worst thing to do is to select people because they represent constituencies; the best is to select those who represent key decision-making categories. One or two people who fit into each of the following categories should be involved in the team:

- Decision maker—someone who is vested with the authority/ responsibility for making a decision related to this change, or someone who has the ear of the decision maker (e.g., key staff member). The literature points out that the more important the problem or change effort, the greater the involvement required of senior staff and administration.
- Stake holder—someone who has a vested interest in how this change occurs; this person will likely be called upon to carry out the decisions made, or at least will be directly affected.
- Expert—someone who has inordinate knowledge about the issue, institution, and/or change process.
- Supporter—someone who is already committed to seeing change occur and has some ideas about potential changes.
- Resister—someone who likes the status quo and is dubious about proposed changes; this is the questioner or gadfly for the team. It would be useful if the person were politically important in the organization.
- Facilitator—someone who has no vested interest in the change but is eager to make the process work. This person should be both task oriented and people centered; skills in collaboration management and meeting facilitation are important here.

In composing the group, one person may represent more than one category, but the whole team should comprise all categories. In forming these teams, you should seek voluntary participation. You cannot compel effective participation; neither can you justly recompense people for it. Released time, when people are free of their usual duties, is often productive, but most change efforts succeed as a result of the passionate belief of willing volunteers, rather than any rewards you offer.

## INITIATING THE TEAM

The first meeting of the team should have no task involvement but should focus solely on team building. Filley (1975) proposes three very productive steps before any problem solving or task endeavors.

### Review and Adjustment of Relative Conditions

At this point, people should introduce themselves and begin to establish trust. Activities that encourage interpersonal sharing and communication should be used.

### Review and Adjustment of Perceptions

This is the time for people to discuss their hidden agendas and hopes/despairs for the change effort. They should also discuss their private grievances and pitfalls. This is a time for reality checks and disclosure.

### Review and Adjustment of Norms/Beliefs

Building on Filley's work, let me propose some beliefs that are particularly conducive to the change and problem-solving process. The team should review these beliefs and add any others they feel are important to the process (see Figure 8.1). The team should also establish norms on how they wish to operate. Some examples of norms are:

- We will keep all team discussions confidential.
- We will operate by consensus, not majority vote.
- We will meet all time lines set by the team.

Both the beliefs and norms should be written on large charts and posted during meetings. While this posting may seem hokey, it acts as a constant reminder of how the group wants to operate and its corporate

We believe that:

1. A change is available to meet all our needs.
2. It is desirable to search for a change that meets all our needs.
3. Cooperation is better than competition.
4. Everyone is of worth in decision making.
5. The views of others are legitimate statements of their positions.
6. Differences of opinion are helpful.
7. Other members are trustworthy.

*Figure 8.1. Beliefs conducive to change.*

beliefs. This process, as well as alternatives to it, stresses two critical elements within the team process: rational and orderly discussion of ideas and the exploration of feelings and values. Both are important to successful change.

## KNOWLEDGE ABOUT CHANGE

One real problem that interferes with team effectiveness is the lack of knowledge about how to create change. Change is like coaching—everyone thinks he knows how to do it, but few can. Eighty percent of the people who watch a Little League game, an AYSO soccer match, or the Dodgers or the Knicks "know" just what it takes to win. If only the coach would . . .! Seldom is it that simple. Our jobs entail more complexities and complications than most casual observers detect.

Change is like that. It is more involved than most of us surmise. Each of us needs to know the research and literature about effecting change. In forming your team you must take early efforts to read about and discuss effective change. Your team needs to operate from a knowledge base.

## PROVIDING RESOURCES

If an ad hoc team is to be successful at creating change, it must have the necessary resources. At this point, let me pose eight resources that are critical to successful team efforts.

## Time

First, change agents need realistic and reasonable time lines. An eager board or an edgy boss may want results in a couple of months, but change takes longer than that. Earlier it was stated that change efforts should have as their planning base one year. A year is long enough to accomplish some things and short enough to sustain interest and commitment. If the change is significant, it may ultimately require three to five years for full implementation; you get there through a series of one-year plans. Undue haste in planning may only elongate the time for implementation and institutionalization.

## Leadership

Each team needs a natural leader. He or she may emerge from within the group or may be supported, but there must be leadership if change is to occur. Kouzes and Posner (1987) found five fundamental practices that enabled "leaders to get extraordinary things done." These leaders

(1) Challenged the process

(2) Inspired a shared vision

(3) Enabled others to act

(4) Modeled the way

(5) Encouraged the heart

Successful change advocates will need to be attentive to these leadership challenges, so as you form a change team, be sure to provide leadership to take up these challenges.

## Discretionary Funds

The power of budgets lies not in their overall size, but in the amount of discretionary funds. If you have a $60 million budget, but only $20,000 in discretionary money, you have little power. Conversely, if you have a budget of only $1 million, but $100,000 in discretionary money, you have significantly more power. Effective change groups need discretionary money to fuel their decisions and reward their ideas. You need to provide your change team with a budget and the discretion to decide on its use. If the CEO or superintendent must approve every expenditure, the change team will not feel they control the money. Give change agents both money and the freedom to use it.

## Freedom

Not all change efforts fall neatly within the lines. In fact, most change efforts violate some established procedures or policies. If you are going to empower a team to pursue change, then you must be prepared to modify standard procedures. This does not mean giving the team carte blanche in all matters, but it does support flexibility in some cases. You must face the reality that as change evolves, it will likely batter and bruise some of your long-lived routines.

Change teams need not only freedom to bend some rules, but also freedom to fail. As noted in Chapter 2, effective change occurs in an environment that promotes experimentation and supports those who dare to go beyond the easily attainable. If you set up an environment in which failure is not accepted, no one will dare to risk.

## Energy and Excitement

Change calls for celebration and excitement. The more you can invest the effort with sparks of energy, the more you will achieve. Find energetic, interested people to join the change team. Most of the trait-based studies of leadership have been shown to have little predictive value (Yukl, 1981; Stogdill, 1981). But a few traits have emerged as critical. Energy is one of these. Little occurs unless individuals have the drive to succeed and the will to overcome resistance. Tired, burnt-out people rarely achieve greatness or create change. Moreover, if team members are to feel energy, verve, and excitement, the leadership of the organization must have those qualities. The team reflects the organizational culture, and the culture reflects the energy and vision of top-level leadership.

## Recognition

Another resource of import is recognition—a prime motivator (Herzberg, 1959). Recognition fuels action and inspires effort. Recognize your change attempt

- at the inception of the team
- periodically during the process
- at the conclusion

This recognition may occur in a variety of ways: at meetings, through notes to individuals, in speeches, etc. The important thing is to recognize the effort.

Let me add a caution, however. Too much recognition may actually be counterproductive. In Chapter 3, I addressed the problem of superiority—the need for all participants to believe they have an equal share in the glory. Thus, in recognizing one particular group or individual, you may unknowingly send a message to others that they are not important, valued, or successful. While moderate tension may produce higher levels of achievement, it can also backfire. Those who feel unrecognized may be so fed up with the team that they have a vested interest in seeing it fail. This negativity is the curse of many a "model" program; the change agents get fragged by the troops.

This dilemma has no simple solution. You must be sensitive to the fine line between reasonable recognition and apparent favoritism. Your best bet is to spread recognition widely throughout the organization.

### Chance to Network

A rich resource for change is the experience of others. It is important to provide the opportunity for a change team to visit other sites, talk to other people, observe the operations of different agencies. Many new ideas evolve from chances to network. At the very least, your team may return with a renewed faith in your own ideas and approaches.

Networking is also important within the organization. Changers need a support base and encouragement from colleagues to try their ideas. The insights of people not directly involved are an invaluable resource to the change teams. Networking, both within and without the organization, provides perspective.

### Empowerment

This last resource is typically the most important. Empowerment occurs when people

(1) Feel their survival is in their own hands
(2) Have important work to do
(3) Sense a clear purpose
(4) Are committed to achieving that purpose

If people are given unimportant work, they feel unimportant and are disempowered. Feeling they have no control over their own survival, they do not seek new possibilities. If they have no purpose, direction, or commitment, they simply react, or even come to a dead stop (Harvey and Drolet, 1994).

Managers who form change teams must empower their teams to move forward. If team members suspect they are merely a dumping ground for a bad idea, lacking any mission or chance of success, they will, in fact, fail. Managers who want vital change need to examine these four factors of empowerment and make sure their team has the resource–power–they need to get the job done.

Ad hoc teams are the best mechanisms for creating effective change. If you form them, equip them, and empower them well, you significantly increase your chances to succeed.

# CHAPTER 9

# Directive Collaboration

THIS chapter focuses on ways of organizing teams to be most effective in creating dynamic change. Effective change is the product of an ability to blend a group of people into strong task achievers. However, a debate rages around this effort.

Some argue that the only way to create change is through collaboration and widespread participation. The accordion process for expanding and contracting participation (see Chapter 6) is a sound approach to emphasizing collaboration. Schmuck and Runkel (1985), Huse (1980), and Bennis (1985) describe other approaches, all of which insist on collaboration.

Others insist, however, that while basically sound, these classic collaborative/consensual approaches are insufficient for the management of most change efforts. They are typically too time-consuming, nondirective, and uncontrollable. They argue for more directive approaches that tell people what to do and when to do it. However, their alternatives, the directive approaches, are equally, if not more, deficient in effect. Both collaborative and directive approaches possess advantages. Combining these advantages markedly increases the probability of successful change.

## ADVANTAGES OF DIRECTIVE MANAGEMENT

Telling people what to do and how to do it has a certain appeal:

- Directive management (DM) works faster than Collaborative Management (CM) because one person manages the process. The manager controls time by establishing a date to begin the change process and by setting the schedule for implementation. Collaborative management, by contrast, requires time to collect multiple inputs and time to resolve the conflicts that often emerge. When time is at a premium, DM is an attractive choice.

- Expertise is explicitly and immediately applied in DM. This management style recognizes that certain individuals possess greater expertise in decision issues—that some team members are more equal than others. Relevant knowledge is brought to bear on the change effort without delay or apology. Collaborative management assumes the worth of each individual and, hence, the inherent equality of each individual in the group. Expertise is accepted only to the point that it is acknowledged as a need by the group as a whole. In some cases, then, CM ignores or rejects useful information. Directive management becomes preferable when specialized knowledge is critical to a high-quality decision.
- Directive management increases control of primary outcomes. The manager tells employees what he or she wants and holds them accountable for getting it done just that way. In collaborative strategies, on the other hand, team members often modify outcomes of the change process. When specific outcomes are critical, DM is preferred.

In summary, DM of change efforts is linear—that is, DM predicts processes, time lines, responsibilities, and outcomes. The manager in DM knows much more about what will happen than the CM manager, who may lose control of those elements of the change effort.

## ADVANTAGES OF COLLABORATIVE MANAGEMENT

Working collaboratively has numerous advantages:

- Collaborative management (CM) is responsive to the participation ethic emergent in most organizations. Naisbitt (1982) and others have pointed out the increasing social urge for participation and involvement in decision making. Collaborative management is highly responsive to this urge.
- Collaborative management shortens the implementation span because team members and those who have been involved through the accordion approach have a higher investment in the change. Simply because of their participation, employees will not fight the change as hard as people subjected to DM.
- A higher level of involvement also increases secondary satisfaction. Participation makes people happier about their jobs. Herzberg et al.'s (1959) satisfiers of achievement, recognition, and responsibility are more fully realized in CM.
- Collaborative management provides more ideas and higher quality

decisions as a result of multiple inputs. Remember the old adage "Two heads are better than one and three heads better than two and . . ." Collaboration elicits broad input, whereas DM tends to suppress it.

In summary, more positive organizational climate emerges as a by-product of participation, investment, job satisfaction, and better decisions. Positive organizational climate increases the probability of future successful change efforts.

## COMBINING THE APPROACHES

Each approach, DM or CM, has advantages, with the advantages of one becoming drawbacks of the other. So why not blend the two into one overall concept—directive collaboration? In this way the manager captures the best of both approaches and increases his chance of effective, long-term change, as shown in Figure 9.1. Under most cir-

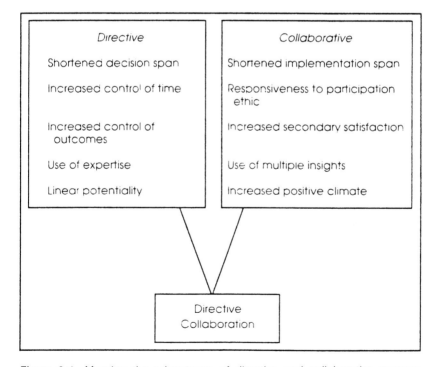

*Figure 9.1.* Merging the advantages of directive and collaborative management.

cumstances directive collaboration is the best approach to managing a change effort.

## DIRECTIVE COLLABORATION STEP BY STEP

The following are the thirteen steps that unite directive and collaborative management into directive collaboration so that the advantages of each cancel the drawbacks of the other.

### Step 1. Include All Sides

An effective change team includes representatives of all key factions in the organization—both those for and against the change. As discussed earlier, when you isolate your enemies, you only strengthen them. Instead, show your commitment to the participation ethic, draw upon multiple insights, and raise secondary satisfaction. Bring your opponents into the process, discover their payoffs, and induce their investment.

Be careful not to form too large a group; five to twelve members make a productive working group. The first step in this process is to form a small change team with perspectives from all sides.

### Step 2. Establish Collaborative Norms/Processes

It is imperative to explain the purposes and processes inherent in collaboration and then to engender buy-in among team members. Filley (1975) provides an excellent example of collaborative norms; any set will do, as long as they are understood and accepted. I recommend allowing one to three hours to discuss group expectations and reach consensus on the norms that will govern the group. By recording the norms on large newsprint sheets and then posting the sheets at each meeting, you will keep group members aware of their agreements. Shared norms facilitate emergence and discussion of conflicting views. Interaction of those multiple inputs will, in turn, yield better decisions.

### Step 3. Define the Problem Domain/Decision Set

Problem definition is a dilemma inherent in many collaborative approaches. Given total freedom to define the problem, a group may spend undue time or misappropriate the real problem. This is a moment for directive collaboration. Before the team gets to work, the manager should define the problem clearly for the group. This is the time for precise explanation of the decision set. What is the question to be answered? What might the recommendation look like? Given such direction, the group is less likely to get off target into side issues. The manager is responsible to know the problem, validate it, then clearly express it to the change team, thus shortening the decision span and maintaining control of outcomes.

### Step 4. Define the Time Frame

Defining the time frame is another directive step. The manager specifies a realistic time frame for results. Ability to set and meet realistic time lines is a major predictor of trust. If I ask for A in June and you deliver, I will be impressed with your dependability. If I ask for A in June and you cannot deliver—if, instead, you explain all your problems and ask for more time—then I will begin to wonder about your dependability. I will begin to doubt.

We all know, also, that work expands to fill time. When that occurs, team members feel that time has been wasted; they feel frustrated. If I tell you that your team will accomplish its task in three meetings, and fifteen are necessary, you lose faith in me.

So giving people a target date and helping them meet it builds your credibility and empowers group members. You increase control of time by providing a time frame.

### Step 5. Define Givens

No change effort operates in a vacuum. Budgetary constraints, political entanglements, facilities restrictions, personal conflicts, and other contextual factors interfere with smooth change processes. The group must understand such givens or constraints so that they can realistically anticipate and work through the reefs and shoals ahead of them. Odysseus would never have survived Scylla and Charybdis without some realistic knowledge of the travails ahead. Forewarned is forearmed. The change manager is responsible to foresee and to describe for the committee its pragmatic boundaries. By keeping the committee on track, this step shortens the decision-making process and helps control outcomes.

### Step 6. Define Unacceptable Outcomes

Not all outcomes are created equal. Some are truly impossible to live with. To refuse explicit recognition of this reality is either naive or self-deceptive. Every team asks, "How much freedom do we have? Will you accept whatever solution or approach we come up with?" You may say yes to this latter question, but few managers mean it. Not that you already have the solution, but you know certain outcomes you cannot accept. If you do not know them, you had better think about the problem. To specify unacceptable outcomes frees the group members to be more creative because they become less concerned with your hidden agenda and more aware of reality.

On the other hand, the manager needs to be open to reconsideration. Your unacceptable outcomes may become desirable with modifications you had not considered. You should avoid premature closure on options that may prove attractive. Nevertheless, defining unacceptable outcomes is a directive step that shortens decision-making time, enhances control of outcomes, and allows richer collaboration on appropriate aspects of the change process.

### Step 7. Reinvent Part of a Wheel

In our eagerness for efficiency, we often urge groups not to "reinvent the wheel." This is poor advice, at least in part. Suppose that you find a host of existing programs or projects and set a change team to figuring out which one to adopt, which one fits best. Probably, none of them really fits. That is why "model programs" have been so unsatisfactory as a vehicle for change.

Therefore, when looking for alternatives, when searching for solutions, it is appropriate to reinvent that which already exists. Although needing more time than simple copying, reinvention increases participation and investment. Create your own wheel out of the spare parts of others. Even though it may not look much different from its predecessor, your new wheel *is* yours, and you own it. Perhaps the whole wheel is not brand new—ideas rarely are—but at least some part of it is yours, and is uniquely suited to your particular situation. So never adopt, always adapt!

### Step 8. Reach for Consensus

Consensus is a deceptively simple notion. Schmuck and Runkel (1985) describe its three essential conditions:

(1) Everyone understands the issue at hand.

(2) Everyone has had a chance to describe how he or she feels about the issue and alternative solutions.

(3) Everyone is willing to go along publicly with the group solution, even though it may not be his or her preferred choice.

True consensus seldom exists, especially relative to point C, but the more closely the group can approximate this condition, the more effective the decision-making process. Consensus approaches avoid voting, averaging, or any other numerical approach because, as mentioned in Chapter 2, these are coercive tactics that increase resistance. Consensus approaches use such tactics as integrative decision making, feeling surveys, stimulation of the minority, and focus delphi (Filley, 1975; Schmuck and Runkel, 1985; and Hencley and Yates, 1974). All these approaches

- encourage participation
- avoid premature closure or selection
- explore feelings
- open members to ideas of others

Consensus is the heart of collaborative management.

### Step 9. Call for Systematic Decision Processes

At this point, after team members have had a chance to explore ideas and possibilities, the manager establishes an expectation that the group will follow carefully considered and well-structured decision processes. Many meetings consist simply of sitting around and discussing matters until everyone seems content. At times this works, but in most cases it does not. To insure exploration and evaluation of all important aspects of the change effort, the team should structure data consideration and decision-making processes more effectively. Useful structuring methods include:

- integrative decision-making model (Filley, 1975)
- trade-off analysis (White, 1985)
- cross-impact matrices (Hencley and Yates, 1974)
- payoff matrices (White, 1985)
- multiattribute analysis (Harvey, 1987)

None of these systems is an automatic pilot system—providing the "answer" to the problem. Each requires human judgment and consideration. What each does, though, is to provide systematic and ordered consideration of information and alternatives. As a consequence, each system is very useful for change issues. Other procedures could be noted; the point is that rational or systematic decision-making processes elicit multiple insights and support a shorter decision span while also enhancing the quality of decisions.

### Step 10. Draw upon Expertise

One of the first exercises in management training for decision making is the NASA survival experiment. (You are stranded on the moon and have fifteen items with you. Which of these items is most useful to your survival? You are to decide individually, and then in a group). This exercise has a host of progeny, all bearing the same moral, "Group decision making is better than solitary decision making," that is, better unless someone has expertise about survival or outer space or whatever topic the decision addresses.

At times, then, group decision making is reduced to pooling collective ignorance. Expertise avoids this, but only if the expert is recognized and used. Therefore, a wise manager insists that the change team use expertise where necessary or appropriate. The team needs to differentiate domains of value from domains of knowledge. Expertise does not help with the former but is essential in the latter. The change team should not become expert dependent; they must rely upon their values and their understanding of the local situation. Direct them to draw upon expertise, but sparingly.

### Step 11. Monitor the Process

No matter how well a process is planned, something is bound to go awry. Hurt feelings, self-doubt, frustration, and/or new realities will emerge. If the team fails periodically to interrupt its task to debrief the process, progress will soon bog down. In our urge to get the job done, we often forget that process affects task. Task behaviors become seductive and all-consuming. We do not want to waste time now talking about the process—"We'll do that later."

Later, however, is too late. Change teams need to pull back periodically, examine how they are operating, and check adherence to their norms. This does not mean that the team becomes an old-fashioned T-group. Nevertheless, feelings are important to task achievement and, hence, must be monitored. Checking the process enhances positive climate, shortens the overall decision-making span, and builds toward smoother implementation.

### Step 12. Air Drafts

This play on words harks back to the accordion process described in Chapter 6. When team members have worked hard and well to develop a proposal, they want closure and finality. They feel good about their achievement and want to celebrate its completion. But premature closure is a fundamental mistake for groups, just as it is for individuals. Moreover, the accordion process reminds us that participation is important at all stages in creating change. Think of your change plan, as well as the change proposal itself, as a looseleaf notebook, not as stone tablets. Pages can be pulled out and put in. Your change is itself open to change.

Insights are generated from an even broader audience as the change team airs drafts at appropriate points along the way. Yes, "drafts" — because this word suggests an incomplete, unfinished document, open to revision. The more chance there is for others to revise, add, and adapt, the more investment will be gained throughout the organization, and, hence, the easier the implementation.

### Step 13. Emphasize Group Credit/Accountability

While every change effort needs a good advocate or two, credit and accountability must fall to the total team. To do otherwise is to undercut the team and weaken potential linkages through the rest of the organization. The last chapter discussed the importance of reducing individual proprietary interest in the change. Emphasizing group credit and accountability are the key step, for you cannot simultaneously toot your own horn and theirs. Group credit fosters positive climate and shortens the implementation span.

## APPLYING DIRECTIVE COLLABORATION

Directive collaboration is particularly useful for, though not limited to, managing change teams. This approach (summarized in Figure 9.1) offers many advantages over either directive or collaborative management alone. Managers find it blends the best of collaboration and directiveness into a healthy and effective management strategy. To support its particular points of strength, a personal example is given (Harvey and Lomeli, 1985).

### Mobile Home Rent Control—The Problem

Excessive rent increases in mobile home parks were plaguing the city of La Verne from 1976 to 1984. Residents registered heated demands for relief, but every time the city council approached the issue, park owners threatened legal suits and the council backed off. In 1984 I convinced the council that I could find a workable solution. The city council unanimously supported my effort to do so.

### Mobile Home Rent Control—The Process

To solve this problem, a task force composed of responsible tenants and park owners was formed. The two sides had never sat together to fight out the issue. I obtained their agreement to norms and procedures. Then I took the strongest step I could—a calculated risk. I told both sides that there *would be* a mobile home rent control ordinance in La Verne, that the issue was not whether there would be an ordinance, but its provisions. I affirmed my intention to create an ordinance that would work for both tenants and owners. But by delimiting the problem to the substance of the ordinance, I avoided repeated philosophical digressions into the propriety of governmental intervention.

I then defined the time frame (four months), the givens (legality and low cost), and unacceptable outcomes (no ordinance). These directive steps set the stage for our deliberations, discussions, and conflicts. We examined several existing ordinances, such as Carson's, Chino's, and Oceanside's. At one point, we brought in an attorney, an expert on rent control, to react to our ideas. Eventually we came to consensus and presented drafts to the city council, mobile home tenants, and park owners one month prior to deadline. The task force then considered all suggestions for revision.

This process was begun in July, 1985, and the ordinance was approved in October, 1985. There have been no legal challenges, and the average yearly cost of administering the ordinance is $800. Additionally, and most tellingly, the park owners have agreed to live with the elements of the ordinance. They are not excited by it, but they can live with it.

| Style | | |
|---|---|---|
| C | 1. | Include all sides. |
| C | 2. | Establish collaborative norms/processes. |
| D | 3. | Define the problem domain/decision set. |
| D | 4. | Define the time frame. |
| D | 5. | Define the givens (political, budgetary, etc.). |
| D | 6. | Define the unacceptable outcomes. |
| C | 7. | Reinvent part of a wheel. |
| C | 8. | Reach for consensus. |
| D | 9. | Call for systematic decision-making processes. |
| D | 10. | Draw on expertise at appropriate points. |
| C | 11. | Monitor/debrief the process. |
| C | 12. | Air drafts. |
| C | 13. | Emphasize group credit/accountability. |

*Figure 9.2.* Thirteen steps in directive collaboration.

## REFLECTIONS ON THE PROCESS

This brief tale highlights several points:

(1) Bringing people together to plan change is critical to effective change. Teams work better than individuals.

(2) Being directive at certain points minimizes misunderstandings and facilitates collaboration on the central issues.

(3) Directive collaboration focuses issues and keeps the change manager in control while also promoting participation and involvement.

For long-term, effective change, I propose directive collaboration, as summarized in Figure 9.2. Try it—you'll like it.

# CHAPTER 10

# Infusing Change into
# Organizational Systems

THE preceding chapters presented and elaborated on a step-by-step team approach to change. Systematic, team-based change processes are relatively uncommon in most organizations. Sometimes managers are already up to their eyebrows in crocodiles. Sometimes the organization refuses to support such a change effort. These are valid reasons for saying, "I like your ideas but I cannot do anything about them just now." But at other times the manager may wish to introduce or expand a systematic team approach to change, yet finds no entry point. In that case, I suggest four likely points of leverage: evaluation, budgeting, strategic planning, and education reform.

## EVALUATION

An array of methods is available for program evaluation (Anderson et al. 1974; Udinsky, et al., 1981; Weiss, 1972). Generally speaking, these involve the following steps:

(1) Selection/definition of evaluators
(2) Selection/validation of criteria for judgment
(3) Data gathering
(4) Data analysis
(5) Reporting

These generic steps outline the phases in an evaluation process, each phase generating cumulative threat and insecurity. Although we protest that a particular evaluation is merely formative and developmental, program participants fear discovery of misdirected efforts or personal inadequacies. Even as it generates insecurity (with an occasional twinge of hope), the evaluation process also consumes resources in the form of time, energy, and money.

Why not take that resource-consuming activity and exploit it to kill two birds with one stone? Why not use the *how* of an evaluation as a mechanism for organizational development and change? Look at the steps described above.

### Selection of Evaluators

The evaluation process begins with selection/definition of evaluators. Let this step serve as the starting point in an effort to infuse change.

Ordinarily, we fall into the trap of seeing data generation as an end in itself. To that end, we hire outsiders or assign neutral insiders to gather information. These evaluators transmit their findings to managers, who usually disregard the report or attend only to those points that confirm their preexisting biases. Most evaluation reports have a dismal record for affecting decisions. This should not surprise us, since we know that rational strategies are the least effective for change (see Chapter 2).

To turn evaluation into the first stage of change, choose a team of interested insiders. Lead team members to view themselves not merely as evaluators but as change agents — to see data gathering as a means of identifying needed changes. When evaluators are interested investigators working toward needed change, then data gathering takes on a new imperative. Forming a combined evaluation-and-change team leads to better, more useable, data.

### Selection of Criteria

Very often, arguments over evaluations center not on data, but on the values represented by the variables. Therefore, the criteria for an evaluation are not the province of an expert or two. Decisions about values require broad-based support. The more everyone in the organization buys into the criteria for judgment, the stronger the findings. If findings are to have impact, you need investment, and participation is the best way to obtain that investment. This is a time to reach out for input and ideas. This is a time for directive collaboration.

### Data Gathering

"Gathering data is just a routine research task," managers often say. But is it routine? For evaluations to receive attention, they must draw upon a wide range of inputs — proponents and opponents, top brass, and grass roots, program leaders and program followers, objective records and subjective feelings, hard data and anecdotal reports—and on and on and on. The more you reflect on all these sources of data, the more you will identify who and what are keeping the program stuck at point A when you want to reach point B.

### Data Analysis

Data analysis is partly a technical task and partly a values task. The values aspect calls for a change perspective. A good evaluation team knows its limitations and recognizes that it may misunderstand reality. Therefore, the team tests its interpretation of the data. It airs drafts and solicits reactions. It seeks participation in the interest both of validity and of later acceptance of the results. It worries about rightness and usefulness, not rightness alone. It cares about change. The *how* of data analysis sets the stage for informed decision making—or predestines the report to a remote file, sealed away with fear and hostility. Evaluation seen as a component of long-term change is more likely to achieve both rightness and usefulness.

### Reporting

It is important to notice the ending on this heading. Report*ing* is more effective than a report. When you tell stories and create metaphors, your audience is more likely to hear you. Remember, data are just a way to portray reality. To be useful, they must be presented dramatically. This final phase in evaluation is not the mechanism for discharging your responsibility, but an opportunity to demonstrate program need and propose change analysis. Many evaluations would be better appreciated if they went beyond recommendations to full-blown change strategies—from descriptions to action plans—for implementation of findings.

In summary, evaluation events are readily transformed into change episodes. By so doing, you alter the side effects of evaluation from psychic hernia to eustress and you move the organization in a positive direction.

## BUDGETING

Budgeting is a perennial evil that managers must endure to survive and promote organizational goals. None of the many alternative budgeting systems is fun. But if budgeting were managed as an opportunity for organizational development and change, it would not only be more effective, but also more enjoyable.

The fundamental elements of budgeting are:

(1) Definition of immediate organizational priorities/goals
(2) Analysis of current fiscal conditions
(3) Analysis of cost/resource implications for the succeeding year
(4) Discrepancy analysis followed by reconciliation of desires with available resources

None of these factors appears on the surface to relate to the change issues I have described earlier, but they do.

### Definition of Priorities/Goals

Definition of organizational priorities and intentions for the succeeding year is an issue partly of maintaining programs, partly of creating change, and partly of resisting or controlling change. An urge to get to the dollar figures should not drive you through this first step too quickly. A good budget manager knows that budgets are only a mechanism for getting things done, not an end in themselves. Budget development becomes enticing and exciting when a clearly delimited time period allows the appropriate organization members to debate:

(1) Which efforts are important to maintain?
(2) What changes do we want to create?
(3) Where do we need controls for changes or environmental demands imposed upon us?

The more thoroughly you explore these questions, the better prepared you will be to encounter the "numbers" with a sense of organizational direction and purpose.

### Analysis of Fiscal Conditions and Resources

The succeeding fiscal analysis, although essentially the task of technical experts, benefits from thoughtful and honest input from managers and line workers. Guided participation, particularly the accordion process described in Chapter 6, insures such input. A second factor that supports change-oriented budgeting is a clear, politically neutral action plan. Finally, unambiguous program objectives facilitate budget choices and reduce subsequent resistance arising from miscommunication.

### Analysis and Reconciliation of Discrepancies

The last phase, analysis and reconciliation of budgetary discrepancies, is the most promising in relation to change. Budget documents seldom inspire organizational acceptance. Even in times replete with resources, budget acceptance is something of a problem. In times of fiscal stricture, such as the post-extravagant era, budget acceptance becomes a critical annual dilemma.

A frequent tactic is to present the budget with the woeful message, "This is the way it has to be. We have no choice—no wiggle room." And everyone leaves disgruntled and resistant. If, instead, a manager were to take budget acceptance as point B of a change effort, and then apply the Change Checklist, a different outcome would ensue. Even if some steps are constrained by time imperatives, the checklist *will* work.

Changee payoff, resistance, and investment are critical issues in budget acceptance. If these are taken into account, organization members *can* feel good about resources and goals for the year ahead, despite tight fiscal strictures. Moreover, the budget process, approached as a problem in change, opens the door to other applications of the Change Checklist.

### STRATEGIC PLANNING

Below (1987) describes six essential elements of strategic planning. Steiner gives a slightly different rendition of steps, with Bryan proposing yet a different array. It would be my proposition to you that the twelve steps illustrated in Figure 10.1 capture the most generic approach to strategic planning. Systematic change strategies share several points in any model.

### Data Analysis/Situation Audit

Establishing need for change is a critical step. The data analysis phase sets the stage as planners assess current conditions and expectations and critique organizational and individual payoff. This analysis

1. Form an appropriate team; garner institutional commitment
2. Establish a Plan to Plan
3. Gather appropriate data (situation audit)
   - SWOT Analysis
   - External expectations
   - Internal expectations
   - Forecasts about future
   - Analysis of present
   - Analysis of past
   - Competitor profile
4. Develop or clarify tenets
5. Create a strategic vision for the organization
6. Examine current programs; develop new programs
7. Identify strategic issues (needs)
8. Formulate strategies for managing issues and programs
9. Devise action plans to manage issues and programs
10. Perform financial projections
11. Review feasibility of vision
12. Monitor progress

(Harvey and Drolet, unpublished)

*Figure 10.1. Steps in strategic planning process.*

would be strengthened by considering strain, valence, and potency; identifying potential actors; and addressing resistance. Moreover, use of these elements would familiarize people with the change process.

### Long-Range and Medium Strategies

In developing long- and medium-range planning, a strategic planner actually engages in change strategies. The planner identifies needed changes and how to achieve them. Then, at the strategy level, a preliminary step of goal prioritization precedes implementation of the Change Checklist. The planner must know first what is important to do, based on previous data analysis, and then apply systematic strategies for change.

### Short-Range Plans

Short-range plans are identical with the action plans described in Chapter 5. They specify who, what, and when in an orderly fashion. In fact, action plans are not peculiar to change but characterize good management, which in turn makes for good change.

Like budgeting and evaluation, strategic planning is rife with opportunities to apply all or part of the Change Checklist. To go even further, strategic and project planning correlate naturally with systematic change processes. Yet, ironically (to take one example), city planners rarely attend to the creation of change. Instead, they focus totally on technical elements of data analysis, logistics, and design. Many a city planner decries the so-called politics of city planning. Often, though, the real problem lies in the planner's own view of the world. He or she fails to conceptualize his role as an architect of problem solving, as a creator of successful long-term change. Hospital planners, facilities planners, and strategic planners in business often make the same error. If all these planners had experience with the Change Checklist (or another systematic approach to change), we would see more responsive, participative planning with fewer delays and turmoil.

## EDUCATION REFORM

I digress at this point to a particular arena for change—education—because it holds particular joy for me. I began and have lived my career in education. While I have worked and consulted in a full array of other, noneducational, organizations, I consistently hear the siren call of education.

Siren, in the other sense of the word, is equally appropriate. For every man, woman, and child in the United States, there is also a theory as to what ails education and what reform is appropriate. Over the last few decades, we have been replete with reform efforts:

- site-based management
- national standards
- school choice
- parent participation in schools
- accelerated learning
- California restructuring grants
- ethnic or gender equity
- magnet schools
- state curriculum frameworks
- Coalition of Essential Schools

- National Diffusion Network
- Comer's School Development Program
- Atlas Project
- tightening of teacher certification
- loosening of teacher certification

Few of these reforms call for the same solution; few derive from the same problem diagnosis, and few are new. This is not a book on reform, so I will not belabor the issue. Let me merely reflect on three elements of reform and relate them to the principles of change.

## Focus

When we researched businesses that had expanded through acquisition, we found two approaches:

(1) Acquiring like enterprises (a shoe company buying other store companies)
(2) Acquiring unlike enterprises (a shoe company acquiring a bank, boutique, or drug store)

We further found that businesses acquiring unlike enterprises were significantly less profitable and productive. The reason? Lack of focus.

Focus creates coherence—the capacity in both employees and clients to know and be committed to what you do (Harvey, Frase, and Larick, 1992). By its nature, education is a defocused organization—education has become the dumping bin for all of society's problems. The solution to all ills is education. Whether the problem be teenage pregnancy, drugs, integration, war, intolerance, or economic despair, education is expected to have a program to fix it. In the process, schools have become defocused, unclear, and often ineffective. The starting point for reform must be system focus. Otherwise, change will go in too many different directions and, hence, will ultimately return to no change (Folk Wisdom 1).

## External

Most educational reforms have not been the product of internal strategies. For the most part, internal approaches have been overridden by external discontent or by the needs of lobby groups. For this reason, more reforms than not have had short lives and yielded checkered achievement. For reform efforts to make real and lasting change, they must grow from a coherent plan developed by both internal and external constituencies. Reform efforts must be

(1) Market-driven — Education must become more market-driven, that is, educators must recognize that they have a customer to whom they must respond. To be market-driven may or may not involve the dreaded voucher plans. Schools can choose to be choice-driven, or choice can be imposed. But competition will and must lead to greater quality.

(2) Smaller and differentiated — To become focused, schools must be more coherent within and more diverse between units. What identifies these units must be clear, and that identification must be valued. The result will be an array of smaller and more differentiated schools.

(3) Well-led — While school leaders need to be responsive to external change demands, they must also have a vision of their own. They must accept higher risk and be more entrepreneurial. In essence, these qualities call for schools to have a strong, consistent change vision built on a variety of ever-shifting, short-term changes.

(4) Strategic — In pursuing change, most reformers have assumed that the power of a good idea is enough. It never is. Rather, you must be as strategic about the *how* of change as the *what*.

To illustrate this point, there is a wonderful group of passionate reformers called the California Science Implementation Network (CSIN). They believe in vitalizing the teaching of science and are rife with ideas. But they also came to realize that their ideas were not enough to effect change, so they started training teachers in change strategies and conflict management. They "got strategic." In the process, they became real reform leaders. For too long, education reform has been built solidly on the what of change; it now needs to recognize the how of change. Reform goes hand in hand with strategic change.

## CONCLUDING NOTE

Myriads of other nooks and crannies, other systems, in your organization would benefit from a more sensitive understanding of change. This chapter has identified entry points for a systematic change process—opportunities for introducing that process to organization members.

Moreover, I have emphasized that change strategies are valuable not just for obvious change efforts, but also for many other normal, day-to-day activities of your enterprise. Therefore, a manager who is also a sensitive, skilled change agent will be more effective in almost every other activity in the organization—a statement bold but true. Have you ever met a good, long-term change agent who was not effective in almost everything he touched?

# CHAPTER 11

# Toward Becoming an Artisan of Change

## IN RETROSPECT

I have now come full circle, back to where I began. The intent of the book was to show you

*how to create change*
*with a simple,*
*but systematic,*
*step-by-step process*

that increases your chance for long-term success. Has it been success-ful? If so, you now know a useful change process and are more alive to the variables that create and control change.

Let me review quickly how to use this process. You start by forming a team. You then move on to the designation of the change effort and establishment of a need. After that, you analyze the situation and de-velop a strategy that takes into account your analysis and findings. Finally, you develop specific action plans and implement your strategy.

That is all there is to change. Sound simple? It really is. In fact, it is critical that you keep the process systematic and simple. That is why I have developed this approach, and why I have written this book. Some years ago I crafted more complex and sophisticated conceptions of change, but I found that they often confused people more than helped them. Now that I am older, I am more impressed with people and systems that help me get something done than with their shining and abstract alternatives. That is why I like old adages and folk wisdom and stories. Good management is less a science than an art form. It is not highly technical, and its knowledge base in no way rivals that of medi-cine, law, engineering, classical languages, or history. But expanse of technical knowledge is not the measure of professional importance. The primary criterion is the degree to which a profession affects the lives of human beings. From this perspective, management is critically important. We need not fabricate obtuse knowledge and vocabulary to elevate it. We need simply to practice better management so as to enrich more lives more fully. We need to be better at our craft, our art.

In the final analysis, this book has attempted to describe better artisanship in management. I am convinced that as managers become more sensitive to change and how to create and control it, they will become better artisans of management generally. In fact, I dare you to follow the advice in this book and also manage poorly. It is like crying and eating or patting your head and rubbing your tummy. It is virtually impossible to do both at the same time. You cannot be a bad manager and a good change agent at the same time.

## FOUR CAVEATS

I want you to keep four caveats in mind as you move toward change artisanship. The first grows out of my own experience but was also aptly identified by Peters and Waterman (1982). This caveat is, "Change requires a bias for action." Not that action alone is sufficient; change also involves analysis and deliberation and strategizing and inclusion. But fundamentally, successful change agents like to get things done. They are bulldogs who will not be distracted by pretty, new fads or discouraging words. When you find one of these rare movers and shakers, exploit to the fullest their bias for action. This bias may not be amenable to training, but it lies dormant in more people than we suspect. When you make a change fun and feasible, you elicit that urge to action.

A second caveat is, "You can change behaviors, but not attitudes." So often, we hope to change people from the "wrong" attitudes or the "wrong" beliefs. But we are doomed. Attitudes are a product of long histories and are not readily changed. Rather, we should seek to alter behavior, and when that behavior is ingrained, attitudes will follow. You cannot make someone feel more collaborative or inclusive, but you can make them behave more collaboratively. We love conversion crises, but seldom see them. We do, however, see behavioral changes.

A third caveat is, "Change is more often a process than a result." The best rendition of this reality is found in C. P. Cavafy's poem "Ithaca." As you probably remember, Odysseus was the great Greek warrior and sage whose journeys were chronicled in Homer's *Odyssey.* Odysseus spent many years in finding his way from Troy to his kingdom and home in Ithaca.

Ithaca

When you start on your journey to Ithaca,
then pray that the road is long,
full of adventure, full of knowledge.
Do not fear the Lestrygonians
and the Cyclopes and the angry Poseidon.
You will never meet such as these on your path,
if your thoughts remain lofty, if a fine
emotion touches your body and your spirit.
You will never meet the Lestrygonians,
the Cyclopes and the fierce Poseidon,
if you do not carry them within your soul,
if your soul does not raise them up before you.

Then pray that the road is long.
That the summer mornings are many,
that you will enter ports seen for the first time
with such pleasure, with such joy!
Stop at Phoenician markets,
and purchase fine merchandise,
mother-of-pearl and corals, amber and ebony,
and pleasurable perfumes of all kinds,
buy as many pleasurable perfumes as you can;
visit hosts of Egyptian cities,
to learn and learn from those who have knowledge.

Always keep Ithaca fixed in your mind.
To arrive there is your ultimate goal.
But do not hurry the voyage at all.
It is better to let it last for long years;
and even to anchor at the isle when you are old,
rich with all that you have gained on the way,
not expecting that Ithaca will offer you riches.

Ithaca has given you the beautiful voyage.
Without her you would never have taken the road.
But she has nothing more to give you.

And if you find her poor, Ithaca has not defrauded you.
With the great wisdom you have gained, with so much experience,
you must surely have understood by then what Ithaca means.
   [C. P. Cavafy, "Ithaca"]

Without Odysseus' journey, there is no epic. His heroic deeds grow out of his voyage, not his arrival. So Cavafy writes:

Always keep Ithaca fixed in your mind.
To arrive there is your ultimate goal.
But do not hurry the voyage at all.
It is better to let it last for long years;
and even to anchor at the isle when you are old,
rich with all that you have gained on the way,
not expecting that Ithaca will offer you riches.

Ithaca has given you the beautiful voyage.
Without her you would never have taken the road.
But she has nothing more to give you.

And if you find her poor, Ithaca has not defrauded you.
With the great wisdom you have gained, with so much experience,
you must surely have understood by then what Ithaca means.
    [C. P. Cavafy, "Ithaca"]

Odysseus neither could, nor would, have wandered without a goal, an Ithaca, but achievement of the goal was not the measure of his heroism. That lay in how he pursued the goal.

With the great wisdom you have gained, with so much experience,
you must surely have understood by then what Ithaca means.

Greatness in planning or change or management lies not in reaching a goal, but in how you journey toward it. Rich, vibrant organizations are those with effective processes. They may not always reach point B; instead they may arrive at $B_1$ or C or $C_1$ or $A_2$. That point may be less or more desirable than the original goal. I strongly believe that a good process increases the probability of a good product, but if I had to choose between the two, I would opt for a process. A good process almost always leads to some good end, even though unintended. Good processes at least yield a positive organizational climate—a pleasant stopping place and a solid foundation for future change.

My final caveat consists of one last bit of folk wisdom. "You can't be a good leader, unless you've been a failure."

Biographies of great leaders and inspired artists reveal that none of them achieved greatness or significant impact without heart-wrenching failures. Their greatness lies not in avoiding failure, but in getting up from it, time after time after time. They kept getting knocked down, and they kept getting up. Edison had thousands of failed experiments for every successful one. Lincoln's life was permeated with obstacles and failings. FDR's greatness emerged from overcoming his impairment. Everyone fails some time, perhaps many times. What marks a good leader, an effective change agent, is not avoiding failure, but rather the capacity to get up and try once more. Change is not a complex task. I have said so again and again. But it does require guts.

# Cited Exercises

## EXERCISE 1. BUTTERMILK: AWARENESS EXPANSION

*Goals*

(1) To demonstrate the processes of interpersonal influence and personal change.
(2) To "warm up" groups that are interested in exploring the dynamics of change.

*Group Size*

A maximum of fifty members.

*Time Required*

One-half hour.

*Materials*

(1) One clean glass.
(?) One unopened quart of buttermilk, injected with blue food coloring.

*Physical Setting*

A circle of chairs with two chairs placed in the middle and a small table placed between the two chairs to accommodate the glass and buttermilk.

*Process*

(1) The facilitator asks who in the group loves buttermilk and who hates buttermilk. One person is selected from each of these groups,

and the two are directed to stand by the chairs in the center of the circle. The remaining participants are instructed to seat themselves in the circled chairs.

(2) The facilitator explains that the lover of buttermilk will have the task of persuading the hater of buttermilk to drink some buttermilk. The unopened quart of buttermilk and the glass are then brought out. (The buttermilk has previously been injected with blue food coloring at the fold of the carton and resealed with candle wax.)

(3) The facilitator advises the person who dislikes buttermilk not to be unduly influenced by the fishbowl situation (i.e., neither unduly resistant and obstinate, nor unduly inclined to yield because of the audience). Rather, he is advised to behave as naturally as possible.

(4) The facilitator instructs the advocate of buttermilk to use whatever verbal techniques he chooses, but not to pour the milk until the resister agrees to try it or the advocate has exhausted all verbal approaches and does not know what to do except to show the resister the milk.

(5) The advocate and resister are told they may stand or sit as they choose, and the process of persuasion is begun. It ends in approximately ten minutes when either the resister agrees to drink the buttermilk and the advocate pours it for him or the resister is obviously not going to try it. At this point, the facilitator suggests that the advocate pour a glass and show it to the resister.

(6) The facilitator leads a discussion of the experience, including

- What was the reaction of the advocate to the buttermilk?
- What does the participants' reaction to the color of the milk say about change processes?
- What different tactics did the advocate use? Which seemed most successful in stimulating change?
- What tactics did the resister use to withstand change? Which seemed most successful?
- What are the differences between demanding/advocating change and accepting change?
- What learnings from this experience can be applied to understanding personal change?

(7) The facilitator gives a lecturette on the dynamics of persuasion and change. He then leads a discussion of the learnings from the experience.

## *Variations*

(1) The physical setting may be altered to make the persuasion process more difficult; for example, the chairs may be set far apart or at awkward angles, or a high table may be placed between them.

(2) Several participants may be allowed to replace one another as advocates or resisters of the buttermilk.

(3) The advocate can speak to the entire group of resisters until he persuades one to comply.

## EXERCISE 2. QUESTIONING EXERCISE

Setting: Group Meeting

Resources Needed: None

Process: This exercise works in the following way:

(1) Ask the group to freeze in its deliberations. This can be done at the beginning of the meeting or any time during it.

(2) Tell the group that for the next thirty minutes no one can initiate a statement. All they can do is:

- ask a question; or
- respond to someone else's question.

(3) Now ask the group to continue in its deliberations.

Result: More listening and more awareness of the needs of others. Overall, there is speedier decision making. Noise in the meeting is significantly reduced.

# *Change Checklist*

## CHANGE CHECKLIST
### (Short Form)

### Analysis

☐   1. Description: What is the change?

☐   2. Potential actors: Who are the changees?

☐   3. Payoff: What's in it for the changee?

☐   4. Unfreezing:

    ☐ Strain

    ☐ Potency

    ☐ Valence

☐   5. Resistance: What are the sources of resistance?

### Planning

☐   6. Change strategy:

    ☐ Rational-empirical

    ☐ Power-coercive

    ☐ Normative-reeducative

☐   7. Resistance strategy: How is resistance to be dealt with?

☐   8. Participation: How is involvement to be generated?

### Implementation and Evaluation

☐   9. Advocates: Who are the visible advocates for the change?

☐   10. Action plan: What are the precise who's, what's, and when's of the change process?

Anderson, S.; Ball, J.; and Murphy, R. T. (1974). *Encyclopedia of Educational Evaluation*. San Francisco: Jossey-Bass.

Barker, J. (1992). *Future Edge*. New York: William Morrow.

Barker, R. G. (1968). *Ecological Psychology*. Stanford: Stanford University Press.

Below, P.; Morrisey, G. L.; and Acomb, B. L. (1987). *Executive Guide to Strategic Planning*. San Francisco: Jossey-Bass.

Bennis, W.; Benne, K.; and Chin, R. (1985). *The Planning of Change*. 4th ed., New York: Holt, Rinehart, and Winston.

Broskowski, A.; Mermis, W.; and Khajavi, F. (1975). "Managing the dynamics of change and stability." In *The 1975 Annual Handbook for Group Facilitators*, La Jolla: University Associates, pp. 173–177.

Burns, J. G. and Stalker, G. M. (1961). *The Management of Innovation*. London: Tavistock Institute.

Chin, R. and Benne, K. D. (1985). "General strategies for effecting change in human systems." In *The Planning of Change*, 4th ed., by Warren Bennis et al., New York: Holt, Rinehart, and Winston. pp. 22–45.

Clance, P. (1986). *The Imposter Phenomenon*. New York: Bantam.

Curtis, M.; Harvey, T.; and Kuhns, E. (1978). *The Institutional Grants Program of the National Endowment for the Humanities: An Evaluation*. Claremont, CA: Project Athena.

Deal, T. and Kennedy, A. (1982). *Corporate Cultures*. Reading, MA: Addison-Wesley.

Devore, D. (1994). "Managing the Force of Positive Stress to Craft Change," unpublished dissertation, University of La Verne.

Drucker, P. F. (1985). *Innovation and Entrepreneurship*. New York: Harper and Row.

Egan, G. (1988). *Change-Agent Skills B: Managing Innovation and Change*. San Diego: University Associates.

England, G. (1992). *A Study for the Validation of the Change Model, Checklist for Change, by Thomas R. Harvey*. Unpublished doctoral dissertation. La Verne, CA: University of La Verne.

Filley, A. (1975). *Interpersonal Conflict Resolution*. Glenview, IL: Scott, Foresman.

Frohman, M. (1970). *An Empirical Study of a Model and Strategies for Planned Organizational Change*. Unpublished doctoral dissertation. Ann Arbor: University of Michigan.

Fullan, M. (1994). *Change Forces.* Alexandria, VA: Association for Supervision and Curriculum Development.

Fullan, M. (1991). *The New Meaning of Educational Change.* New York: Teachers College Press, Columbia University.

Goodman, P. and Associates (1982). *Change in Organizations.* San Francisco: Jossey-Bass.

Hage, J. and Aiken, M. (1970). *Social Change in Complex Organizations.* New York: Random House.

Hall, G. E. and Hord, S. (1987). *Change in Schools: Facilitating the Process.* Albany, NY: SUNY Press.

Harrison, E. F. (1981). *The Managerial Decision-Making Process.* 2nd ed., Boston: Houghton-Mifflin.

Harvey, T. (1979a). "Blue buttermilk." In *The 1979 Annual Handbook for Group Facilitators.* La Jolla, CA: University Associates.

Harvey, T. (1979b). "Transactions in the change process." In *The 1978 Annual Handbook for Group Facilitators.* La Jolla, CA: University Associates.

Harvey, T. (1987). *Multi-Attribute Analysis.* Unpublished monograph. La Verne, CA: University of La Verne.

Harvey, T. (1975). Staffing and organizational development. In *Strategies for Sufficient Survival,* by Clifford Stewart and Thomas Harvey, San Francisco: Jossey-Bass.

Harvey, T. and Drolet, B. (1994). *Building Teams, Building People.* Lancaster: Technomic.

Harvey, T.; Frase, L.; and Larick, K. (1992, June). Can school leadership transform to face the future? *School Administrator,* 49:8–13.

Harvey, T. and Lomeli, M. (1985). "Problem-solving approach nets workable solution to rent control dilemma." *Western City,* LXI:10–13.

Havelock, R. (1970). *A Guide to Innovation in Education.* Ann Arbor: Institute for Social Research.

Hafferlin, J. B. L. (1969). *Dynamics of Academic Reform.* San Francisco: Jossey-Bass.

Hencley, S. and Yates, J. (1974). *Futurism in Education: Methodologies.* Berkeley: McCutchan.

Herzberg, F.; Mausner, B.; and Snyderman, B. B. (1959). *The Motivation to Work.* New York: Wiley.

Hodgkinson, H. (1971). *Institutions in Transition.* Berkeley, Carnegie Committee Report. New York: McGraw-Hill.

Huse, E. (1980). *Organization Development and Change.* Los Angeles: West Publishing.

Isaac, S. and Michaels, W. B. (1984). *Handbook in Research and Evaluation.* San Diego: EDITS.

Jellison, J. M. (1993). *Overcoming Resistance.* New York: Simon & Schuster.

Jones, J. (1972). "Spiro Model." In *1972 Annual Handbook for Group Facilitators.* La Jolla, CA: University Associates.

Jones, J. and Bearley, W. (1986). *Organizational Change Orientation Scale – OCOS.* Bryn Mawr: Organizational Development and Design.

Kanter, R. M. (1983). *The Change Masters.* New York: Simon and Schuster.

Kast, F. and Rosenzweig, J. (1985). *Organization and Management: A System and Contingency Approach.* New York: McGraw-Hill.

Kirkpatrick, D. (1985). *How to Manage Change Effectively.* San Francisco: Jossey-Bass.

Kouzes, J. M. and Posner, B. Z. (1987). *The Leadership Challenge.* San Francisco: Jossey-Bass.

Lewin, K. (1951). *Field Theory in Social Science.* New York: Harper and Row.

Lippitt, G.; Langseth, P.; and Mossop, J. (1985). *Implementing Organizational Change.* San Francisco: Jossey-Bass.

Lucas, R. and Harvey, T. (1984). "Successful strategies for institutionalizing grants." *Grants Magazine,* 7:19–24.

Maslow, A. (1970). *Motivation and Personality.* New York: Harper and Row.

McCelland, W. (1968). *The Process of Effecting Change.* U.S. Department of HEW Professional Paper, pp. 32–68.

Naisbitt, J. (1982). *Megatrends.* New York: Warner.

Odiorne, G. (1981). *The Change Resisters.* Englewood Cliffs, NJ: Prentice-Hall.

Peters, T. and Austin, N. (1985). *A Passion for Excellence.* New York: Random House.

Peters, T. and Waterman, R. (1982). *In Search of Excellence.* New York: Harper and Row.

Pfeffer, J. (1981). *Power in Organizations.* Marshfield, MA: Pittman.

Pfeiffer, J. W. and Jones, J. E. (1978). "OD readiness." In *1978 Annual Handbook for Group Facilitators,* La Jolla: University Associates, pp. 219–226.

Schein, E. (1979). Organizational socialization and the profession of management. In *Organizational Psychology,* by David Kolb et al., Englewood Cliffs, NJ: Prentice-Hall.

Schmuck, R. and Runkel, P. (1985). *The Handbook of Organization Development in Schools.* 3rd ed., Palo Alto, CA: Mayfield.

Scriven, M. (1967). "The methodology of evaluation." In *Perspectives of Curriculum Evaluation.* AERA Monograph series on Curriculum Evaluation, #1, Chicago: Rand-McNally.

Seyle, H. (1975). *Stress without Distress.* Philadelphia: Lippincott.

Stake, R. (1967). The countenance of educational evaluation. *Teacher College Record* 68:523–40.

Steiner, G. (1979). *Strategic Planning: What Every Manager Must Know.* New York: Free Press.

Stogdill, R. M. (1981). *Handbook of Leadership.* New York: The Free Press.

Stufflebeam, D. L.; Foley, W. J.; Gephart, W. J.; Guba, E. G.; Hammond, R. L.; Merriman, H. O.; and Provus, M. M. (1971). *Educational Evaluation and Decision-Making.* Itasca, IL: Peacock.

Suchman, E. (1967). *Evaluative Research.* New York: Russell, Sage.

Tosi, H.; Rizzo, J.; and Carroll, S. (1986). *Managing Organizational Behavior.* Marshfield, MA: Pittman.

Udinsky, F.; Osterbind, S.; and Lynch, S. (1981). *Evaluation Resource Handbook.* San Diego: EDITS.

Weiss, C. (1972). *Evaluating Action Programs.* Boston: Allyn and Bacon.

White, M. J.; Clayton, R.; Myrtle, R.; Siegel, G.; and Rose, A. (1985). *Managing Public Systems.* Lonham, MD: University Press of America.

Yukl, G. (1981). *Leadership in Organizations.* Englewood Cliffs, NJ: Prentice-Hall.

Zaltman, G.; Florio, D.; and Sikorski, L. (1977). *Dynamic Educational Change.* New York: Free Press.